Spooktacular Tales

Spooktacular Tales

25 Just Scary Enough Stories

Dianne de Las Casas

Illustrated by Soleil Lisette

An Imprint of ABC-CLIO, LLC

Santa Barbara, California • Denver, Colorado

Copyright © 2016 by Dianne de Las Casas

All rights reserved. No part of this publication may be reproduced, stored in a retrieval system, or transmitted, in any form or by any means, electronic, mechanical, photocopying, recording, or otherwise, except for the inclusion of brief quotations in a review, without prior permission in writing from the publisher.

Library of Congress Cataloging-in-Publication Data

Names: De Las Casas, Dianne, author.
Title: Spooktacular tales : 25 just scary enough stories / Dianne de Las Casas.
Description: Santa Barbara, CA : Libraries Unlimited, 2015.
Identifiers: LCCN 2015031633 | ISBN 9781440836909 (paperback) | ISBN 9781440836916 (ebook)
Subjects: LCSH: Supernatural. | Horror tales. | Storytelling. | BISAC: LANGUAGE ARTS & DISCIPLINES / Library & Information Science / Collection Development. | LANGUAGE ARTS & DISCIPLINES / Library & Information Science / General.
Classification: LCC GR500 .D435 2015 | DDC 808.8/037—dc23 LC record available at http://lccn.loc.gov/2015031633

ISBN: 978-1-4408-3690-9
EISBN: 978-1-4408-3691-6

20 19 18 17 16   1 2 3 4 5

This book is also available on the World Wide Web as an eBook.
Visit www.abc-clio.com for details.

Libraries Unlimited
An Imprint of ABC-CLIO, LLC

ABC-CLIO, LLC
130 Cremona Drive, P.O. Box 1911
Santa Barbara, California 93116-1911

This book is printed on acid-free paper ∞
Manufactured in the United States of America

For Mary Jo Huff,
A friend to the end,
No bones about it!
—Dianne de Las Casas

For Eliana,
My little sister with a big heart
I love you, "Silly-ana!"
—Soleil Lisette

Contents

Introduction ix

Why Tell a Scary Story? 1
    Various "Scarious" 3
        Jump Tales 3
        Legends 3
        Urban Legends 3
        Ghost Stories 3
        The Gory Story 4
        Slightly Spooky 4
    How to Determine Age Appropriateness of Your Story Selection 4
        Pre-K and K (Ages 3–5) 4
        Grades 1–3 (Ages 6–8) 4
        Grades 4–6 (Ages 9–12) 5
        Grades 7–12 (Ages 13–18) 5
    Establishing an Environment of Trust 5
    Storytelling with Pacing, Timing, Pitch, and Tone 6
        Pacing 6
        Timing 6
        Pitch 6
        Tone 6
Thirteen Tips for Telling Spooky Stories 7

The Scary Stories

The Spook-O-Meter 13
Aaron Kelly's Bones 15
Baba Yaga 19
Bloody Mary 23
Bone Soup 26
The Brown Suit 30

The Call from the Grave 32
Creak, Crack, Thump, Bump! 35
The Crying Baby 38
The Curse of Pele 40
The Ghost of John 42
The Ghost with One Black Eye 46
Ginny Greenteeth 49
The Graveyard Bone 52
The Hairdo 55
The Hook 57
I'm Coming for Your Soul! 59
Irish Eyes 61
It Floats! 64
La Llorona (The Wailing Woman) 67
Over in the Graveyard 69
Pulling the Pumpkin 72
The Sack Filled with Treats 75
Sneakers 78
The Tinker and the Ghost 80
The White Satin Gown 83

Source Notes 85
Web Resources 89

Introduction

There is nothing like the thrill of a good ghost story! I've been telling scary stories for a long time. It started in elementary school. I loved giving my younger brother the "heebie-jeebies" by telling him a good ghostly tale. I'd lie in his room in the top bunk while he was in the bottom bunk. I'd tell him stories about the monster that lived underneath the bed. Inevitably, he would climb into the top bunk and then I would leave! Then there were the Scouts. As a Scout, you learned the art of spooky telling when you went camping with your troupe. Many of the stories I tell today are from my childhood.

Spooktacular Tales is a follow-up to the ever-popular *Scared Silly: 25 Tales to Tickle and Thrill* because children love a good spooky story. It's like a roller-coaster ride. They adore the thrill of the chill. Yet, at the end of the ride, the children know they are safe. I have written this book as another "primer" on telling scary stories. In addition, there are 25 spooky tales. Many are storytellers' classics. Each story is annotated with suggestions on how to tell the tale. What makes this book different from other scary story anthologies is I have given each of the stories a rating by the "Spook-O-Meter," which determines how scary a story is. It is designed this way so that you, as a storyteller, can determine the age and grade appropriateness of each story.

It's time to get ghostly and enjoy some *Spooktacular Tales*!

Warmly,

Dianne de Las Casas
dianne@diannedelascasas.com
www.diannedelascasas.com

Why Tell a Scary Story?

Telling a scary story is a fine line to walk. Many audience members, particularly elementary and middle school–age children, will beg for scary stories but yet, when you tell them, you may hear protests from angry parents. In his web article "What's Scary Enough?" celebrated storyteller and musician Odds Bodkin suggests, "Kids only rejoice in scariness when deep down they feel safe and know it's not real. Scariness tickles a safe child in a fun way, but it deepens real fears in an unsafe child. So know who's in your audience. Offer the option for those who would rather not listen to leave."

The key is to know your child. Some souls find scary stories disturbing, even at mature ages. The question arises whether dwelling in this sensitivity to things macabre too long—rather than coming to terms with life's scariness early—is good or not. But that's a decision only you can make.
—Odds Bodkin, professional storyteller and author

Richard and Judy Dockery Young, authors of *The Scary Story Reader* and *Favorite Scary Stories of American Children*, say, "Children love scary stories and, in fact, benefit from them by facing and mastering the little moments of 'fear for fun' these tales provide. Naturally, every storyteller needs to know the audience and judge the appropriateness of every frightening folktale."

> *With every story comes responsibility. You are responsible for the stories you share. Don't neglect your responsibility. Sometimes a story that has grotesque and senseless violence is not one to share with others. Don't choose your stories like a shopping list; choose like it will affect someone, because it will. You determine the outcome by not only your telling, but your story choice.*
> —Kevin Cordi, professional storyteller

In the introduction to *Haunted Bayou and Other Cajun Ghost Stories*, the late J. J. Reneaux stated, "The ghost stories in this collection have been passed down from generation to generation through storytelling. They have served not only as entertainment but as teaching tools, helping tellers and listeners remember the legends, myths, and history of their people. They have also acted as warnings, cautioning against the dangers of breaking rules and taboos of society. Now as then, tales of ghosts provide comfort by allowing people to face their worst fears without true danger."

Diane Ladley, who is known as "America's Ghost Storyteller," explains the dynamics of fear and says that how the brain uses fear as a means of signaling danger is a way to maximize the chances of survival in a dangerous situation. Diane says scary stories:

- Provide a safe way to exercise and develop our fear system.
- Teach appropriate actions and options to choose from.
- De-sensitize us to scary things to help us cope—habituation.
- Sensitize us to real-life fearful situations and build caution.

> *Kids need make-believe violence to help them cope with real-life dangers.*
> —Diane Ladley, America's Ghost Storyteller

Roberta Simpson Brown, author of *Queen of the Cold-Blooded Tales*, offers this explanation as to why she believes stories have value, "When I became a professional storyteller, I realized that one thing all human beings have in common is the powerful emotion of fear. I saw that scary stories grabbed the attention of the most reluctant listener. When I look out at the huge audiences that come to hear ghost tales, I am convinced that people have a need to share fear and realize that they are not alone."

> *Telling stories is something people have done for thousands of years, for most of us like being scared in that way. Since there isn't any danger, we think it is fun.*
> —Alvin Schwartz, author of *Scary Stories to Tell in the Dark*

Fear is one of the world's most universal emotions. Every culture has ghost stories. The value of telling a scary story becomes apparent when you witness a group of children beg for more spooky stories after you've just finished telling a ghostly tale. When children realize that other children share their trepidation, their place in the story audience becomes a safe place within which to process their fears.

Various "Scarious"

It is important to know the various types of scary stories that exist. Familiarizing yourself with the different types of scary stories will enable you to build a larger repertoire of stories suitable for all age ranges.

Jump Tales

These are stories that are usually told with a "Gotcha!" at the end, a story with a surprise ending intended to make audiences jump. They are great for older elementary kids, sharing around a camp fire, or at a sleepover. Examples of jump tales include "Bone Soup," and "Creak, Crack, Bump, Thump!" The late, great Jackie Torrence said, "But when you tell a Jump Tale, remember that the expressions in your face and your gestures are what children watch, but your whole body is telling the story. You must put all of yourself into it."

Legends

Legends are stories that are born out of actual events. The stories eventually become so big and exaggerated that they turn into legends. An example would be "The Legend of the Sleepy Hollow."

Urban Legends

American kids love urban legends. These are stories that originated in or around urban or city areas. Urban legend origins are usually difficult to trace. People always claim that urban legends are "absolutely true" because they heard it from a friend or another reliable source. A good example of an urban legend is "The Ghostly Hitchhiker." Urban legends are great for older audiences such as teenagers.

Ghost Stories

Ghost stories are those tales of the supernatural in which ghosts are sighted or play a major role. There are tales of hauntings in which spirits are said to roam the earth. Other ghost stories are tales that truly send chills up the spine. Many people claim that their ghost stories really happened. The stories from the Myrtles Plantation in St. Francisville, Louisiana (purported to be one of America's most haunted houses) are a great example.

The Gory Story

These tales are what I consider "slice and dice" horror and not at all appropriate for early childhood and elementary-age children. These types of stories are full of gratuitous violence and are often the fodder of teen horror flicks.

Slightly Spooky

These spooky tales are designed with the younger ones in mind. They draw out the suspense and spookiness until the end of the story when the storyteller delivers a funny punch line. Many of these types of stories had their beginnings as jokes. They are also referred to as "Shaggy Dog" stories. Good examples include "Rap, Rap, Rap," "The Viper," and "The Coffin."

How to Determine Age Appropriateness of Your Story Selection

How old should a child be to listen to a scary story? First, it depends on your definition of "scary." Second, age appropriateness is very subjective and is dependent on the child's maturity level. Finally, it depends on the "permissions" of your audience, the types of scary stories they are *expecting* to hear.

That being said, I like to follow some general guidelines when telling stories. If you are billing your scary storytelling program as a "family program," then it needs to be age-appropriate for the youngest audience member. You need to deliver stories that work well with all ages.

Pre-K and K (Ages 3–5)

At this age, children are often easily frightened and have a low tolerance for fear. Many children at this age are afraid of Santa Claus and the Easter Bunny. Stories told to this audience should be short, silly, fun, and participatory. Characters should be exaggerated and cartoony.

Grades 1–3 (Ages 6–8)

Children at this age have developed a larger fear of the unknown. They are afraid of the dark, invisible monsters in the closet, creatures under the bed, and things that go bump in the night. They are also likely to jump into bed with their parents if they are truly frightened. Scary stories for this age group should be suspenseful, silly, animated, and slightly spooky. "Shaggy Dog" tales and jump stories work well with this group.

Grades 4–6 (Ages 9–12)

These children are testing their boundaries and their limitations. They are often heavily influenced by their peers. They are no longer "babies" and purport to "not be afraid of anything." They want their friends to think they are "cool." Don't let their brave facades fool you. They still get scared! They purposely choose scary story books because they enjoy the thrill of the adrenaline rush. With this age group, you can venture into more complex stories with intricate plot twists, psychological thrills, and scary stories. Suspenseful stories with lots of creepy sound effects and jump tales work well. Though they are older children, it is important to assuage their fears at the end of the storytelling session, letting them know that they are safe.

Grades 7–12 (Ages 13–18)

Kids at this age love to be truly frightened. These are the young adults that play "truth or dare," often asking for the "dare." They enjoy "true" ghost stories, gory stories, and stories that deliver a psychological "high speed chase." They like white-knuckled, edge-of-your-seat terror. Good examples of classic stories for this age group are "The Monkey's Paw" and "The Tell-Tale Heart."

Establishing an Environment of Trust

Fear is a funny thing. For children, an environment of "shared fear" such as a roller-coaster ride, a frightening movie, or a scary storytelling session can actually act as a bonding agent and help build an environment of trust. Children will huddle together, hold hands, and cover each other's eyes and ears, even when they don't know each other!

But you have to be very careful. As the storyteller, you hold all the power in your voice, your face, and your body. One wrong turn can send your audience careening down Chaos Chasm. It is your responsibility to give your audience a thrill ride yet return them safely to the ground.

You can establish trust with your audience through your body language. Smiling and open body language draws people in. Animated, cartoon-like characters appeal to smaller children. Large gestures, loud voices, frightening faces, and "Hulk-like" body movement cause audiences to shrink. Know when to be bold and when to pull back. Carefully watch your audience's reaction. Intense fear and anxiety will cause tears, widened eyes, dilated pupils, shallow or rapid breathing, and closed body language such as covering the eyes and sticking fingers in the ears.

Storytelling with Pacing, Timing, Pitch, and Tone

Telling spooky tales is all about pacing, timing, pitch, and tone ("PTPT"). These are a storyteller's secret weapons. Learn how to master "PTPT," and you will be able to control your audience's reaction when telling tales that tickle and thrill.

Pacing

Pacing is how fast or slow the story moves when you tell it. If a boy is running away from something through the woods, the pacing of your voice (your words) should be fast to indicate urgency. On the other hand, if the boy is tiptoeing to peek inside a house, your voice should move at a slower pace to indicate creeping and sneaking. Pacing a story just right, so that it is told neither too fast nor too slow, is vital in keeping your audience's attention.

Timing

Timing in a story is very important. Timing allows your listeners to process what they are hearing. It also allows the storyteller to deliver lines effectively, creating tension, drama, suspense, and relief. In the story of "The Viper," the last line depends entirely on timing. When delivered properly, the entire audience erupts in simultaneous laughter. Silence or a dramatic pause can add more suspense and tension in a story than trying to fill the space with words. Saying "It was just the wind . . . (BIG PAUSE) or was it?" allows readers to ponder that question. To get a sense of timing, listen to a joke with a good punch line. How the punch line is delivered is dependent upon the comedian's sense of timing.

Pitch

The pitch of your voice are the highs and lows of your vocal notes. You can carry your listeners on a rising crest or set them down gently in a falling tide. Your pitch can be as bold as a thunder bolt or as timid as a light drizzle. You can create characters within a story through your pitch. A high-pitched voice could be that of a mouse, while a low-pitched voice could be that of a lion.

Tone

When I speak of tone, I refer both to the tone of your voice and your story. Your story's overall tone has the power to influence your audience. A story such as "Going on a Ghost Hunt" will need a cartoony, comic tone because it is meant for a young audience, while a story such as "The Ghostly Hitchhiker" can begin in a more ominous tone, foreshadowing the suspense and tension of the story.

Thirteen Tips for Telling Spooky Stories

1. Know Your Audience

If you are telling to a mixed age group, stories should be appropriate for the youngest member of your audience unless the program has been advertised otherwise. Select stories that are appropriate for the age group to whom you are telling. A too-scary story can result in disaster. A story that is too "babyish" for an older crowd will cause your audience to lose interest.

2. Adjust Your Space

If you are telling to a mixed group, arrange the seating so that smaller children are with older siblings, parents, or grandparents. Arrange the children so that they are sitting in a close cluster—this makes for a more ambient telling and makes children feel safer when they are in a group. If appropriate, dim the lights.

3. Permission to Leave

Give audience members permission to leave if they find the story too spooky. Sometimes, children will sit through a tortuous storytelling session because they do not know it is okay to leave. It is nice to have an alternate space for these children—an area where they can play or color.

4. Spooky or Scary?

Know the difference! Children need to know what they are getting when it comes to spooky stories. Are you telling spine-tingling tales or super scary stories? Let your audience know so that they have the option to leave.

5. Comforting Ritual

Sometimes, a comforting or silly ritual can help assuage children's fears. For instance, you can say to the children: "If you get too scared later, do this [*Show children a raspberry with your mouth and have them repeat it*] and say: 'I'm not afraid!'" (*Wildly wave pointer finger side to side*).

6. The Tale's Title

Feel free to adapt the stories to suit your personal storytelling style. That's what storytellers do. When choosing a title for your tale, create a title that does not give the story away. For example, in my book, *Scared Silly: 25 Tales to Tickle and Thrill*, I changed "The Nail in the Attic" to "The Attic" because "The Nail" gave away the punch line of the story.

7. Audience Participation

Audience participation makes a scary story not so scary because the children also become the tellers of the tale. It gives them ownership of the story and ownership is power. It also provides a distraction from the terror their imaginations can invoke. Try telling "It Floats" without audience participation and you will see a completely different audience. It can be a downright terrifying tale. On the other hand, adding a participatory refrain allows children a break from their natural tendency to turn simple fear into terror.

8. Sound Effects

Sound effects can be a very effective device in adding a spooky ambience to a tale. Great sound effects for scary stories include howling winds, creaking doors, footsteps, scratching, growling, knocking, thumping, and other loud, creepy noises. If you invite the children to participate in the spooky sound effects (this is great for younger children), it becomes less scary for them.

9. The Bell Curve

When putting a scary story program together for a mixed age group, generally follow a bell curve. Warm up with a not-so-scary story, gradually increasing the intensity of the suspense and thrill. Reach the peak with a spine-tingling, hair-raising tale and then decrease the intensity by ending with a funny spooky tale, joke, or song. Remember to announce to your audience that your stories will be increasing in intensity so that people have the option to leave if they wish.

10. Suspense and Relief

For children, listening to a scary story is about suspense and relief. Build the suspense in your stories, creating tension and drama but be sure to provide a vehicle for release and relief. Children, especially, need to know that they are okay at the end of a scary story.

11. Voice, Face, and Body

The use of your voice, face, and body is essential in telling scary stories. They all work together to persuade and influence your audience. Don't be afraid to exaggerate expressions and add vocal variety when telling to children. Use your body to create characters and denote scene changes. Consistently block your space. If you have an imaginary table on your right-hand side, it should always stay that way.

12. Audience's Reaction

Gauge your audience's reaction when telling your stories. Be prepared to scale back your telling if your audience shows an undue amount of fear or anxiety. External signs of distress include tears, widened eyes, dilated pupils, shallow or rapid breathing, and closed body language (covering eyes or plugging ears).

13. Bringing the Audience Home Safe

As storytellers, it is our responsibility to make sure our audience is safe, especially when the audience consists of children. End a program with a funny story, joke, song, silly antic, or chant such as, "Give yourselves a big pat on the back. Our tales are done and that is that."

The Scary Stories

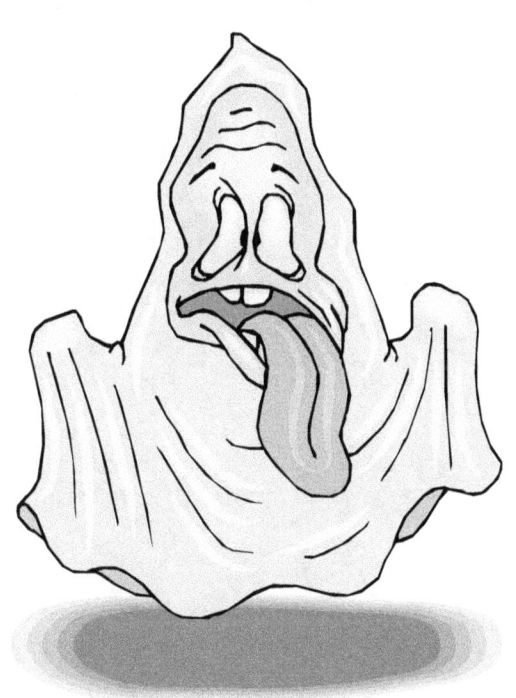

The Spook-O-Meter

The Spook-O-Meter graphic throughout the book is designed to help you to gauge the appropriateness of the story for your audience. When telling scary stories, you can always tell "up" but not "down." That means that stories appropriate for younger audiences can be told to older audiences; however, stories for older audiences are not usually appropriate for younger audiences. There are times when I allow you to make adjustments to the story to change its "Spook-O-Meter" factor. Stories in the Spook-O-Meter 2 range are the best stories to tell for a multi-age audience such as mixed grade levels and family audiences.

Fun and silly. Stories are appropriate for ages 3–5 or grades PK–K.

14 \ Spooktacular Tales

Slightly spooky, humorous, and suspenseful. Stories are appropriate for ages 6–8 or grades 1–3. These stories work for a family audience as well because of the humor.

Spooky and spine-tingling. Stories are appropriate for ages 9–10 or grades 4–5.

Super spooky and bone-chilling. Stories are appropriate for ages 11–13 or middle school.

Super duper spooky. Stories are appropriate for the bravest of souls.

Aaron Kelly's Bones

Ages 9-10, Grades 4-5

Note from Dianne: This old African American tale from the South has a humorous element to it. Aaron dies but he does not feel dead so he gets up and goes home. What happens after that can be as comical and as animated as you wish.

Aaron Kelly died. His widow dressed him in his best attire, bought him a coffin, and had him a nice funeral. He was buried in the cemetery not far from the house.

But that night, Aaron Kelly, bones and all, got out of his coffin and walked home. His widow and his family were sitting around the fire. They were astonished when he walked in and sat down in his favorite rocking chair. [*Make a surprised face.*]

He said, "What are you all looking at? Why are you acting like someone died?"

His widow responded, "Someone did die, Aaron. And that someone is . . . [*pause*] YOU." [*Point to an imaginary Aaron or single someone out from the audience.*]

Aaron Kelly said, "I don't feel dead. I feel fine."

His widow replied, "But Aaron, you are dead. Now get yourself up and get back in your coffin."

Aaron Kelly retorted, "I am not going back to the cemetery until I feel good and dead. So there." He continued to rock in his chair. [*Motion rocking back and forth.*]

From *Spooktacular Tales: 25 Just Scary Enough Stories* by Dianne de Las Casas. Illustrated by Soleil Lisette. Santa Barbara, CA: Libraries Unlimited. Copyright © 2016.

But like Aaron Kelly's widow said, he *was* dead. In fact, his old bones were dry and stiff. His bones CREAKED and they CRACKED as he rocked and rocked. [*Emphasize "creaked" and "cracked" as sound effects and make a rocking motion.*] It was getting sooooo annoying!

One day, a fiddler came to town. He had heard that Aaron Kelly died and he had his eye on Aaron's widow for quite some time. Aaron Kelly's widow invited the fiddler inside.

Little did the fiddler know that Aaron Kelly was indeed DEAD [*emphasize "dead"*] but he was still there. Aaron Kelly was in his rocking chair. His bones CREAKED and they CRACKED as he rocked and rocked. [*Emphasize "creaked" and "cracked" as sound effects and make a rocking motion.*]

The fiddler said, "Well, I can't very well marry you if this dead corpse keep creaking and cracking all day and all night long."

Aaron Kelly said, "I am not going back to the cemetery until I feel good and dead. So there." He continued to rock in his chair. [*Motion rocking back and forth.*] His bones CREAKED and they CRACKED as he rocked and rocked. [*Emphasize "creaked" and "cracked" as sound effects and make a rocking motion.*]

The fiddler said, "Well, I might as well get to fiddling."

Aaron Kelly, "Good! Let's dance!" So the fiddler played a tune and Aaron Kelly began to dance. [*Do a dance here, being as comical as you wish.*]

He shook 'dem bones to the left

He shook 'dem bones to the right

He was a'creakin' and a'crackin'

While the fiddler made a racket

All day long and into the night.

Aaron Kelly's bones clicked and clicked, and suddenly, one of his femurs flew off. Aaron's widow said to the fiddler, "Play faster!"

So the fiddler played a tune and Aaron Kelly began to dance. [*Do a dance here, being as comical as you wish.*]

He shook 'dem bones to the left

He shook 'dem bones to the right

He was a'creakin' and a'crackin'

While the fiddler made a racket

All day long and into the night.

Aaron Kelly's bones clicked and clicked, and suddenly, two of his humerus bones flew off. Aaron's widow said to the fiddler, "Play faster!"

So the fiddler played a tune and Aaron Kelly continued to dance. [*Do a dance here, being as comical as you wish.*]

He shook 'dem bones to the left

He shook 'dem bones to the right

He was a'creakin' and a'crackin'

While the fiddler made a racket

All day long and into the night.

Aaron Kelly's bones clicked and clicked, and suddenly, one of his femurs flew off. Aaron's widow said to the fiddler, "Play faster!"

So the fiddler played a tune and Aaron Kelly continued to dance. [*Do a dance here, being as comical as you wish.*]

He shook 'dem bones to the left

He shook 'dem bones to the right

He was a'creakin' and a'crackin'

While the fiddler made a racket

All day long and into the night.

Aaron Kelly's bones clicked and clicked, and suddenly, three of his phalanges flew off. Aaron hopped and he bopped while his old bones dropped. The fiddler fiddled and Aaron Kelly fell to pieces until the only thing left was his head.

Aaron Kelly head said, "I am not going back to the cemetery until I feel good and dead. So there." His head continued to shake, rattle, and roll. [*Shake hands in front of you, rattle hands above your head, and roll hands in front of you.*] His head CREAKED and it CRACKED as he rocked and rolled. [*Emphasize "creaked" and "cracked" as sound effects and make a rocking motion.*] It was still sooooo annoying!

The fiddler couldn't take it anymore. He packed up his fiddle and said to the widow, "Peace out, girl scout!" [*Say this in a funny way.*] The fiddler never came back.

Aaron Kelly's family gathered up his old, crickety crackety bones and buried him . . . [*pause*] again. This time, they mixed up his bones so he couldn't put them back together. After that, Aaron Kelly stayed in the cemetery.

As for his widow? Well, word got around about her husband, the dancing skeleton [*Shake your arms.*] and no suitors came a'knockin' after that. All because Aaron Kelly creaked and cracked. And that was that.

Baba Yaga

Ages 9-10, Grades 4-5

Note from Dianne: "Baba Yaga" is a Russian folktale. Because it has a "witch" in the story, I've rated it a "3" on the Spook-O-Meter. There is audience participation in this tale, which decreases the level of spookiness. It's also more adventurous than spooky. I like to create a "girl" voice for Natasha and an "old woman" voice for Baba Yaga.

On the other side of yesterday, there lived a mother and her daughter, Natasha. One day, Natasha's mother needed a needle and thread [*Mime needle and thread.*] to mend the clothes.

She said to her daughter, "Natasha, I need you to visit the home of Baba Yaga. Please ask nicely to borrow a needle and thread."

Baba Yaga was a wicked witch, as wicked as they come. [*Make a witchy face and bend your "gnarled" fingers.*] She lived in a hut built on dancing chicken legs. [*Do a silly dance.*] She rode around in a mortar, steering with her pestle. [*Mime flying in a mortar and steering with a pestle.*] Worst of all, she had teeth of metal and LOVED for children to be her . . . dinner! [*Pause dramatically before "dinner."*]

Natasha was afraid but she was a dutiful daughter. Natasha's mother gave her a basket filled with a stick of butter, a piece of meat, and a hunk of bread. Natasha traveled long and far and finally reached Baba Yaga's hut on dancing chicken legs. [*Do a silly dance.*]

The hut was behind a long fence with a great gate. When Natasha pushed through the gate, it creaked and moaned in agony. [*Make a creaking and moaning sound.*]

Natasha said, "Poor gate. You need your hinges greased." She took out the stick of butter and rubbed it on the gate's hinges. [*Mime rubbing butter on a gate.*] It opened quietly and allowed Natasha to pass. [*Mime a gate opening with your hand.*]

Natasha came upon a skinny dog in the yard. The dog growled. "Poor dog. You need some food." She took out the piece of meat and fed it to the dog. [*Mime feeding a dog.*] The dog gobbled it up quickly and appreciatively. He wagged his tail [*Wag your "tail."*] and allowed Natasha to pass.

A scrawny cat sitting near the hut mewed pitifully. "Poor cat. You need some food." She took out the hunk bread and fed it to the cat. [*Mime feeding a cat.*] The cat gobbled it up quickly and appreciatively. She purred [*Make a purring sound.*] and allowed Natasha to pass.

Baba Yaga sniffed the air. A child was near! She poked her head out of the window. "What do you want, little girl?" she asked as she licked her lips.

Natasha answered, "My mother has sent me to borrow a needle and thread." [*Mime needle and thread.*]

"Come in then, child." The hut on chicken legs bent down and allowed Natasha inside.

Then Baba Yaga ordered, "Now get in the tub and wash yourself. I want you clean when I cook you for my dinner!" Baba Yaga locked Natasha in the bathroom.

Natasha began to cry. A voice spoke, "Do not cry, little girl. I will help you." It was the scrawny cat. "You were kind to me so I will help you. Fill the tub and splash around but don't get in." [*Make splashing sounds.*]

Natasha nodded and did as she was instructed. She filled the tub with water and splashed. [*Make splashing sounds.*]

Baba Yaga yelled through the door, "Are you washing yourself?"

Natasha answered,

"Splishy, splash

Splashy splish

I'm washing up

Just as you wish." [*Invite audience to join in.*]

"Good." Baba Yaga went outside to collect wood for her stove.

While Baba Yaga was gone, the cat said, "Now take this mirror and comb. When you are in trouble, throw the mirror behind you. When you are in trouble again, throw the comb behind you. Now climb out the window."

So Natasha ran as fast as her little legs would carry her. [*Mime running.*] When she came to the dog in the yard, he happily gave Natasha a ride to the gate. The dog said, "You were kind to me so I will help you."

When she came to the gate, the gate happily swung wide open for her. [*Mime a swinging gate with your hand.*] The gate said, "You were kind to me so I will help you."

Meanwhile, Baba Yaga returned to the hut. She yelled through the bathroom door, "Are you washing yourself?"

The cat answered,

"Splishy splash

Splashy splish

I'm washing up

Just as you wish." [*Prompt audience to join in.*]

But Baba Yaga grew impatient. "You are taking too long. I shall cook you now." She opened the door only to discover the cat bathing inside the tub.

Baba Yaga screamed, "Cat, why did you not stop the girl?"

The cat answered, "All these years you've been mean and only threw me scraps to eat. The little girl fed me well so I helped her."

Baba Yaga was angry. [*Act and sound angry.*] She ran outside and said to the dog in the yard, "Dog, why did you not stop the girl?"

The dog answered, "All these years you've been mean and only threw me scraps to eat. The little girl fed me well so I helped her."

Baba Yaga was furious. [*Act and sound furious.*] She ran all the way to the gate and screamed, "Gate, why did you not stop the girl?"

The gate answered, "All these years you've been mean and never once oiled my hinges. The little girl greased me well so I helped her."

Baba Yaga was enraged. She ran so fast that she nearly caught up to Natasha. Natasha looked back and saw Baba Yaga right behind her. She reached into her pocket and pulled out the mirror. [*Mime pulling out a mirror.*] She threw it behind her and a deep river formed between her and Baba Yaga. [*Wave arms in front of you to symbolize a river.*]

Baba Yaga screamed, "I'll get you still!" Baba Yaga ran back to the house and hopped into her mortar. She floated across the river, using her pestle as an oar. [*Mime floating in a mortar and steering with a pestle.*] Soon, Baba Yaga caught up to Natasha.

Natasha looked back and again saw Baba Yaga right behind her. She reached into her pocket and pulled out the comb. [*Mime pulling out a comb from your pocket.*] She threw it behind her and a tall forest formed between her and Baba Yaga. Baba Yaga could not even fly over it. Behind the cage of trees, Baba Yaga was trapped. She stomped her feet and pulled her hair. [*Stomp your feet and pull your hair.*]

Natasha ran all the way home into the arms of her mother. [*Mime running.*] She told her mother the story and never again [*Wiggle pointer finger back and forth to signify "never again."*] did Natasha have to borrow a needle and thread from the wicked and mean Baba Yaga. [*Make a witchy face and bend your "gnarled" fingers.*]

Bloody Mary

Note from Dianne: When I was in junior high, my friends and I would dare each other to go into the bathroom, close the door, and stand in the dark, chanting, "Bloody Mary" three times. Legend has it that if you conjure Bloody Mary in the mirror, she will . . . well find out by reading the story. This one's a spooky one that can cause nightmares so tell it with discretion.

There was once a queen who was the most vicious queen around. She ruled with an iron hand and if people disobeyed her or made her angry, she chopped off their heads. [*Make a "slicing" motion with your hand across your throat.*] Just like that. Many lost their lives at her hands and when Queen Mary finally died, they say that she died in a room filled with mirrors. Her spirit got trapped in the reflection and since that time, she has been trying to claw her way out. Her legend has grown. She is known as . . . [*pause*] "Bloody Mary."

Tina and her friends loved playing tricks on each other and daring each other to do outrageous things. One night, Tina had a sleepover and had three of her best friends over. They called themselves the Alpha Squad because they were the smartest girls in the class. Her bestie, Bailey, suggested that they play some games. "How about charades?"

Cassidy, the pushiest personality of the group said, "Boring." [*Draw the word out as you say it.*] "I think we should play 'Bloody Mary.'"

Tina said, "No way. I'm not playing. There's dumb, dumber, and dumbest. And that is the dumbest idea ever." [*Speak with exaggerated junior high "drama."*]

Lauren asked, "What's Bloody Mary?"

All three girls whipped their heads around to stare at Lauren. [*Stare in disbelief.*]

Bailey asked, "You've never heard of the game?"

Lauren shook her head. [*Shake your head no.*]

Tina said, "You go into the bathroom in the dark and call out "Bloody Mary" three times. If she appears, she slashes you and you die. So no, we are not playing this silly game." [*Cross arms and look indignant.*]

Cassidy laughed, "So, Tina, are you chicken?"

Tina said, "I'm just not playing. That's all."

Bailey said to Cassidy, "Well, since YOU suggested it, why don't YOU be the first to play? We'll stand outside the door. Unless, of course, YOU are chicken!" [*Emphasize "you."*]

The three girls stared at Cassidy. She huffed, "Fine. I'm NOT afraid and I will go first!"

The girls walked to the guest powder room, which had a giant mirror but no windows. When the door was shut, it was completely . . . [*pause*] dark.

Cassidy stepped inside and Bailey pulled the door shut. Lauren yelled, "Don't turn on the light. We can see it underneath the door."

Cassidy sighed. [*Let out a deep sigh.*] She never actually played before and she couldn't believe she was the one in the bathroom. *I can do this* she thought.

Bailey yelled, "Hurry up in there, Cassidy. We don't have until tomorrow!"

Cassidy retorted, "Be quiet so I can concentrate!" Cassidy's eyes adjusted to the darkness she saw her faint reflection in the mirror. *It's just a silly childhood game. I'll be fine.*

Cassidy closed her eyes and began chanting, "Bloody Mary." She said it loud enough so that her friends could hear. "Bloody Mary." She said it louder. "Bloody Mary." Still louder. [*Each time you say "Bloody Mary," escalate the pitch and intensity of your voice.*]

Then . . . [*pause*] nothing. She opened her eyes and began laughing. "I did it!" she yelled.

Suddenly, Cassidy saw a reflection in the mirror and it wasn't her own. She screamed. [*SCREAM for the jump effect.*]

Tina yelled, "That's not funny, Cassidy!" Tina, Bailey, and Lauren flung the door open. There on the bathroom floor, was the lifeless body of their friend. She had slash marks across her throat and on the mirror were the words . . . [*Pause for dramatic effect.*]

BLOODY MARY. [*Emphasize "Bloody Mary" with gravity.*]

Bone Soup

Ages 3–5, Grades PK–K

Note from Dianne: This is a great cumulative story to do with the very young. To "de-scarify" the story, I have them participate in the story with me, allowing them to remember all the ingredients that go into the soup. You can even "mix it up" by asking the audience for ingredient suggestions. Even if you don't prompt them to participate, they will naturally do so.

An old woman was traveling a long way. She passed by a graveyard and saw a big fat bone. She decided to pick it up and put it in her bag. [*Mime putting a bone in a bag.*]

A little while later, she came upon a village. She was very hungry and asked the village people if she could have a bite to eat. The townsfolk didn't want to share their food because they had so little of it so the woman came up with a plan.

She went into the middle of town and built a big fire. Someone lent her a pot and some water. She dropped in the bone. The old woman cried out, "Bone soup! Bone soup! I am making bone soup!" [*Chant in a sing-songy voice and invite the audience to participate.*]

Soon, the villagers came to watch. The old woman said, "I know you're hungry so I'll share."

An old man laughed, "How will you make a soup out of that?"

The old woman replied, "It's a magic bone and it will make a magical soup." She took a sip. [*Mime sipping the soup.*] "Very tasty but it needs something else!"

A little boy stepped forward, "I have a potato. Can you use that?" The woman nodded yes. [*Nod yes.*]

She dropped in the potato right next to the bone

The bone in the pot, ready to boil. [*Invite audience to recall ingredients.*]

The old woman cried out, "Bone soup! Bone soup! I am making bone soup!" [*Chant in a sing-songy voice and invite the audience to participate.*]

She took a sip. [*Mime sipping the soup.*] "Very tasty but it needs something else!"

A little girl stepped forward, "I have a carrot. Can you use that?" The woman nodded yes. [*Nod yes.*]

She dropped in the carrot right next to the potato

and dropped in the potato right next to the bone

The bone in the pot, ready to boil. [*Invite audience to recall ingredients.*]

The old woman cried out, "Bone soup! Bone soup! I am making bone soup!" [*Chant in a sing-songy voice and invite the audience to participate.*]

She took a sip. [*Mime sipping the soup.*] "Very tasty but it needs something else!"

A young lady stepped forward, "I have an onion. Can you use that?" The woman nodded yes. [*Nod yes.*]

She dropped in the onion right next to the carrot

and dropped in the carrot right next to the potato

and dropped in the potato right next to the bone

The bone in the pot, ready to boil. [*Invite audience to recall ingredients.*]

The old woman cried out, "Bone soup! Bone soup! I am making bone soup!" [*Chant in a sing-songy voice and invite the audience to participate.*]

She took a sip. [*Mime sipping the soup.*] "Very tasty but it needs something else!"

A young man stepped forward, "I have a bulb of garlic. Can you use that?" The woman nodded yes. [*Nod yes.*]

She dropped in the garlic right next to the onion

and dropped in the onion right next to the carrot

and dropped in the carrot right next to the potato

and dropped in the potato right next to the bone

The bone in the pot, ready to boil. [*Invite audience to recall ingredients.*]

The old woman cried out, "Bone soup! Bone soup! I am making bone soup!" [*Chant in a sing-songy voice and invite the audience to participate.*]

She took a sip. [*Mime sipping the soup.*] "Very tasty but it needs something else!"

A mother with two children stepped forward, "I have a head of cabbage. Can you use that?" The woman nodded yes. [*Nod yes.*]

She dropped in the cabbage right next to the garlic

and dropped in the garlic right next to the onion

and dropped in the onion right next to the carrot

and dropped in the carrot right next to the potato

and dropped in the potato right next to the bone

The bone in the pot, ready to boil. [*Invite audience to recall ingredients.*]

The old woman cried out, "Bone soup! Bone soup! I am making bone soup!" [*Chant in a sing-songy voice and invite the audience to participate.*]

She took a sip. [*Mime sipping the soup.*] "Very tasty but it needs something else!"

The old man stepped forward, "I have some ham. Can you use that?" The woman nodded yes. [*Nod yes.*]

She dropped in the ham right next to the cabbage

and dropped in the cabbage right next to the garlic

and dropped in the garlic right next to the onion

and dropped in the onion right next to the carrot

and dropped in the carrot right next to the potato

and dropped in the potato right next to the bone

The bone in the pot, ready to boil. [*Invite audience to recall ingredients.*]

The old woman cried out, "Bone soup! Bone soup! I am making bone soup!" [*Chant in a sing-songy voice and invite the audience to participate.*]

She took a sip. [*Mime sipping the soup.*] "Very tasty but it needs something else!"

A skeleton missing a bone stepped forward. He said, "I need my bone back. It's my humerus bone and without it, I'm not funny." The woman nodded yes. [*Nod yes.*]

She reached into the pot where she . . .

dropped in the ham right next to the cabbage

and dropped in the cabbage right next to the garlic

and dropped in the garlic right next to the onion

and dropped in the onion right next to the carrot

and dropped in the carrot right next to the potato

and dropped in the potato right next to the bone

The bone she pulled out of the pot, which had already boiled. [*Invite audience to recall ingredients.*]

She returned the humerus bone to the skeleton, who danced a jig and told jokes all night as the entire village feasted on Bone Soup. Bone [*pause*] Appetit!

The Brown Suit

Ages 9-10, Grades 4-5

Note from Dianne: "The Brown Suit" is a slightly spooky story that has a funny ending. This story is fun to exaggerate the crying of the woman in the story. I also like to play up the ending with the "What the?!!!" factor.

A woman had just lost her husband and had to go to the funeral to check on last minute details. When the mortician showed the woman her husband in the coffin, she began blubbering. [*Exaggerate crying with blubbering and "nose blowing."*]

The mortician said, "I'm so very sorry for your loss. I know how hard it must be to lose your husband of so many years."

The woman wiped her nose with a handkerchief. [*Motion wiping your nose and sniffle.*] "Oh, I am sad but that's not why I am crying. My husband looks hideous!" [*Motion toward the "coffin."*]

The mortician apologized. "I'm so sorry ma'am. Is it his hair? I can fix it . . . I looked at pictures and he looks much like he did when he was alive."

The woman sniffled and wiped her nose again. [*Motion wiping your nose and sniffle.*] "Oh no. You did a great job. It's just that my husband would NEVER wear a polka dotted suit! When he was alive, he wore a plain old, boring brown suit." [*Emphasize "plain," "old," and "boring."*]

The mortician smiled. "Oh good. I mean, I can fix that quite easily. Give me a few moments."

A little bit later, the mortician returned with the coffin. The man was in a brown suit. The woman looked inside the coffin, satisfied.

The woman said, "I'm sorry to be such a bother. I know how much time it must have taken to switch the clothing on two bodies."

The mortician smiled. "Oh no! It was no bother at all. I simply switched the heads!" [*Laugh.*]

"You what?" [*Do an exaggerated hands-on face expression while looking at the audience.*]

The Call from the Grave

Ages 9-10, Grades 4-5

> *Note from Dianne:* This is a great campfire story and one that is perfect for a mixed group of adults and kids. I've updated it to modernize it a bit because kids can now relate to cell phones. There is a saying, "When the dead call, don't answer." However, in this case the call from beyond results in a surprising twist.

Sophie was completely grief-stricken. She was a young widow with a baby. [*Mime rocking a baby in your arms.*] Even though she lost her husband, John, three months before, she was still inconsolable. [*Give a big, heavy sigh and look forlorn.*] John was a good guy. Everyone liked John. He was captain of his neighborhood football team, he was president of the home owners association, and he was a firefighter.

On an uneventful day in March, [*Lower voice and then escalate the pitch with more excitement.*] a fire ignited in a house just a few blocks away from where Sophie and John lived. The fire spread quickly and blazed through the house. A mom and her daughter were trapped . . . [*dramatic pause*] inside the house! John's buddy, Mike, saved the woman but the little girl was still stuck inside the burning building! John grabbed his gear and although his captain told him it was too late to enter the house, John went inside anyway. The captain was right! It was too late. [*Lower voice to a somber note.*] John died in the fire. He lost his life trying the save the life of another.

At the urging of her sister, Sophie began boxing up John's things. [*Mime placing items in a box.*] She came across his cell phone. [*Place hand to ear and create the gesture for a phone.*] She still had the service on and kept the phone charged. The screensaver was a picture of their family: John, Sophie, and then newborn, Sidney. Sophie knew her sister was right. John wasn't coming back. It was time to move on. She took the batteries out of the phone and placed the phone inside her dresser drawer. [*In one fluid motion, mime opening the dresser drawer, placing phone inside, and closing the drawer.*]

It was a hot day in June and the weather forecasters said that a big storm system was approaching. Sophie placed all of the boxes that had John's clothes in it, in the garage. Sidney was napping so she decided to sit down, have a glass of lemonade, and relax. She sat in John's favorite chair and began reading. [*Mime opening a book.*]

Suddenly, Sophie heard thunder crash. It was so loud that it made her jump and woke up Sidney, who started crying. The wind howled. [*Make a howling wind wound.*] Rain pounded against the roof. [*Clap hands against thighs to create the sound of "rain."*] As soon as Sophie picked up the baby, her cell phone rang. She dashed into the living room but didn't answer it in time. It went to voicemail. Then, the phone rang again. This time, she answered it.

"Sophie, get down into the basement now. A tornado is coming!" urged a faint but distinct voice.

"John?" asked Sophie incredulously. [*Make a surprised face.*]

The voice yelled, "There's no time. Go into the basement NOW!" [*Raise voice at the word "now."*]

Sophie was shocked to hear her dead husband's voice on the line. Nevertheless, she listened to her gut . . . [*pause*] and the dead voice, and took baby Sidney into the basement. She and Sidney crouched in the far corner of the basement as the storm raged. It sounded like a freight train roaring overhead. [*Make a loud roaring sound.*] Sophie prayed and protected her child as the tornado RIPPED [*Say this loudly.*] the house off its foundation. Rubble fell all around.

A few hours later, Sophie heard a man yelling, "Over here! Over here!" She recognized the voice. It was Mike, her husband's best buddy at the fire station. Mike cleared the rubble and found Sophie huddled underneath, cradling baby Sidney. They were fine but Sophie was in shock.

Mike pulled them out and couldn't believe his eyes. "Sophie, do you realize how lucky you are? Look at this . . ." [*Make a sweeping gesture with your arm.*]

Sophie looked around and saw nothing but rubble. The tornado destroyed everything. Sophie answered, "Yes, I know. It was John who saved my life."

Mike said, "What? What do you mean? Sophie, John is gone . . ." [*Say this is a grave tone.*]

Sophie replied, "He called me just seconds before the tornado hit and told me to go into the basement. I know his voice, Mike. It was John."

Mike shook his head no. "Sophie, I know how hard this is but John is really gone."

Sophie became indignant. "I'm not crazy, Mike. I know what I heard!" [*Raise voice.*]

Mike shrugged. "Okay, Sophie. I have lots of work to do here but first, I'm going to take you to the cemetery to show you that Mike is gone for good."

Mike and Sophie rode to the cemetery in the small, backup fire truck. They walked to John's grave. They couldn't believe what they saw . . . [*Lower voice and pause for dramatic effect.*]

On top of the grave was John's cell phone. It was on. The screen flashed the family picture. Sophie picked it up and checked it. The batteries were still . . . [*pause*] gone. Then Sophie remembered that she missed a call. She checked the voicemail and put it on speaker for Mike to hear.

"Sophie, it's John! I'll always be watching over you and Sid . . . So get into the basement . . . NOW!" [*Say this with urgency.*]

Mike's face looked like he had seen . . . [*pause*] or heard . . . [*pause*] a . . . [*pause*] GHOST! [*Say this LOUD for the jump effect.*]

Creak, Crack, Thump, Bump!

Ages 9-10, Grades 4-5

> *Note from Dianne:* This is a fun campfire story and plays with sound effects. I love the jump at the ending. The trick to this story is to amp the man's growing nervousness and to really play up the sounds. It has the flavor of Edgar Allen Poe's "The Tell-Tale Heart" in a much milder form.

A man was sitting in his worn leather chair, reading his favorite book. The room was silent save for the soft crackle of the fire burning in the fireplace.

"Creeeeeak." [*Draw out the sound of "creak."*] A faint distant sound echoed in the distance.

"Crack!" [*Say this quickly and loudly.*] Something snapped. Was it the sound of trampling?

"Thump!" [*Say "thump" in a deep voice.*] Was something dragging on the ground?

"Bump!" [*Say "bump" in a big, deep voice.*] Where was that big bad noise coming from?

The man ignored the ominous sounds and just kept on [*pause*] reading. The room was silent save for the soft crackle of the fire burning in the fireplace.

"Creeeeeak." [*Draw out the sound of "creak."*] The sound echoed closer to the house. Was it the neighbor's house?

"Crack!" [*Say this quickly and loudly.*] Something snapped nearby. Perhaps it was a small animal?

"Thump!" [*Say "thump" in a deep voice.*] The dragging sound was closer. Maybe a branch was hitting the roof?

"Bump!" [*Say "bump" in a big, deep voice.*] Where was that big bad noise coming from?

Unable to ignore the sounds any longer, the man stood up and peeked out of the window. There was no wind. There was no rain. A bright, full moon hung in the inky sky. Laughing at his own nervousness, the man sat back down in his worn leather chair and just kept on . . . [*pause*] reading.

"Creeeeeak." [*Draw out the sound of "creak."*] The sound was right next to the house. Was could possibly creak like that?

"Crack!" [*Say this quickly and loudly.*] Something snapped right outside. It sounded bigger than a small animal. . . .

"Thump!" [*Say "thump" in a deep voice.*] The dragging sound at the door. Why was he alone tonight?

"Bump!" [*Say "bump" in a big, deep voice.*] Where was that big bad noise coming from?

The man stared into the fire, trying to calm his frazzled nerves. But that didn't calm the sounds. [*Say the following faster and with more urgency.*]

"Creeeeeak." [*Draw out the sound of "creak."*]

"Crack!" [*Say this quickly and loudly.*]

"Thump!" [*Say "thump" in a deep voice.*]

"Bump!" [*Say "bump" in a big, deep voice.*]

The sounds were louder. The sounds were at the door. The man was scared but he had to find out what was out there . . . [*Say the following faster and with more urgency.*]

"Creeeeeak." [*Draw out the sound of "creak."*]

"Crack!" [*Say this quickly and loudly.*]

"Thump!" [*Say "thump" in a deep voice.*]

"Bump!" [*Say "bump" in a big, deep voice.*]

Slowly, he opened the door. . . . [*Pause and then make a drawn-out creaking sound.*]

[*SCREAM for the jump effect. Then pause dramatically for a few seconds.*]

[Say softly.] The room was silent save for the soft crackle of the fire burning in the fireplace.

The Crying Baby

Ages 11-13, Middle School

Note from Dianne: "The Crying Baby" is a tale that is told all over the South and in the Appalachian Mountains. It is also known as "The Rosewood Casket." There are many stories like this floating around the Internet. I actually found a true story very similar to this. Because there is a lifeless baby in the story, the story is a bit chilling.

Mary and Joe had a large family and had just welcomed a new addition. [*Create a "cradle" in your arms and motion back and forth.*] Baby Sarah was beautiful but fragile. It wasn't five days after Baby Sarah was born that she took sick. Her face was as pale as ivory, her lips were as blue as a twilight sky, and she had a raging fever. Although Mary and Joe called the doctor right away, by the time the doctor came to the house, it was too late. Baby Sarah had stopped breathing. [*Lower voice and sound solemn.*]

Mary and Joe were heartbroken. Joe did the best he could and took an old family heirloom table, and turned it into a beautiful casket. Mary cut a piece of lace from her wedding dress she was saving and wrapped it around her cold, stiff baby. [*Motion the wrapping of the lace.*] They laid the lifeless infant inside the coffin and buried her on a cold, gray day.

Mary became inconsolable. She stopped caring for her other children and took to the bed. She couldn't make herself get up and she rocked back and forth, [*Do a rocking motion.*] crying her eyes out. Joe tried comforting her but Mary was completely grief-stricken. Finally, Mary fell asleep with a piece of the lace in her hand.

From *Spooktacular Tales: 25 Just Scary Enough Stories* by Dianne de Las Casas. Illustrated by Soleil Lisette. Santa Barbara, CA: Libraries Unlimited. Copyright © 2016.

Suddenly, Mary bolted upright in bed. She screamed, "Joe, I hear the baby crying!" [*Say this very loudly, startling the audience (at your discretion).*]

Joe replied, "Mary, you know that's not possible. We buried our sweet Sarah yesterday. She's gone. The baby is gone."

After an hour of convincing Mary that she was just dreaming or imagining things, Mary fell back asleep. [*Put both hands together and place them next to your face to convey sleeping.*]

A little while later, Mary sat up in bed again. She yelled, "Joe, I hear the baby crying!" [*Say this very loudly, startling the audience (at your discretion).*]

Joe tried to argue otherwise but Mary insisted she wasn't imagining things. "Joe, I hear our daughter crying. She needs us. We must go to her. We must visit . . . the graveyard." [*Pause dramatically and then say, "graveyard."*]

Joe finally agreed to take Mary to the cemetery. He said, "When you see that Sarah is finally gone, will you let go of this crazy notion?"

Mary nodded yes. [*Nod yes.*] Joe woke his oldest daughter to watch the other children while they were gone. They climbed into their carriage and rode to the town's graveyard. Joe and Mary walked to the tombstone where they had laid their infant daughter to rest. Ever so faintly, there was a cry . . . [*You can either allow the room to be silent here or make a faint crying sound.*]

Mary said excitedly, "See? I told you."

Joe was nervous. He said, "Mary, I don't know if this is such a good idea. You don't know what we will find inside that casket."

Mary was furious. [*Express anger.*] "What do you mean?! Our BABY is inside that casket! We have to dig her up." Mary ran to the carriage and grabbed a shovel.

Joe took the shovel from Mary and began digging . . . [*Pause dramatically.*]

There, they found it. The casket. They opened it up and . . . [*Pause dramatically and lower your voice.*] There was the baby, lying lifeless, wrapped in lace, inside the little casket that Joe made.

WAAAAAAAAH! [*Give a loud baby-like cry, startling the audience.*]

The Curse of Pele

Ages 9-10, Grades 4-5

Note from Dianne: I spent a portion of my childhood living in Hawaii. There, I heard countless tales of Hawaiian gods and goddesses. Pele, the goddess of Mt. Kilauea, the volcano on the big island of Hawaii, is a goddess with a fiery temper. She controls the volcano and one must always respect her spirit. Read what happens to those who don't . . .

In the great Hawaiian islands, the people tell the story of a curse. The curse of Pele, the goddess of fire.

Pele and her sister, Namaka, who is the goddess of the sea, did not get along. They had a fight so big that Namaka chased Pele around the Hawaiian islands, always putting out her fire. Pele finally retreated to the big island of Hawaii. There she dug a fire pit in a high spot, and made it deep so that not even her sister, the sea goddess, could dampen her spirit. [*Mime digging a fire pit.*]

Namaka decided that she could not destroy her sister so she let Pele be. Ironically, it was not the huge quarrel between the two sisters that turned Pele forever bitter and angry. It was because of a . . . [*pause dramatically*] man. It is said Pele became involved with a man called Fire-Eater. When he turned his attentions to another woman, Pele found out and became enraged. [*Make a mad face.*] She turned him into a fish called the humunuku-nukuapuaa. [*Place hands in front of you palms facing the floor. Place one hand on top of the other, forming a "fish." Make your "fish" "swim."*] Since then, Pele has become bitter and temperamental.

From *Spooktacular Tales: 25 Just Scary Enough Stories* by Dianne de Las Casas. Illustrated by Soleil Lisette. Santa Barbara, CA: Libraries Unlimited. Copyright © 2016.

Locals say that Pele is very protective of her island. Tourists are warned not to remove any black lava sand or lava rock from the island. You must even shake every last grain of it from your shoes if you go to the black sand beach. [*Shake feet.*] There are dire consequences for those who decide to defy Pele's wishes and take her volcanic rock and sand home with them . . . [*Lower your voice.*]

When people take Pele's sacred volcanic rock and sand home with them, bad things happen. A string of bad, no, horrendous luck begins. People lose jobs, get divorced, get injured, lose loved ones, and even die. [*Emphasize each phrase.*] The problem is so bad that, every year, the Hawaiian post office receives thousands of packages from tourists returning what they took from Pele, with a note asking for forgiveness. [*Place hands together in front of you, fingers to the ceiling.*]

The next time you visit Hawaii, enjoy its endless beauty but leave it where it belongs or you too may encounter the wrath, the Curse of Pele! [*Say in an ominous voice.*]

The Ghost of John

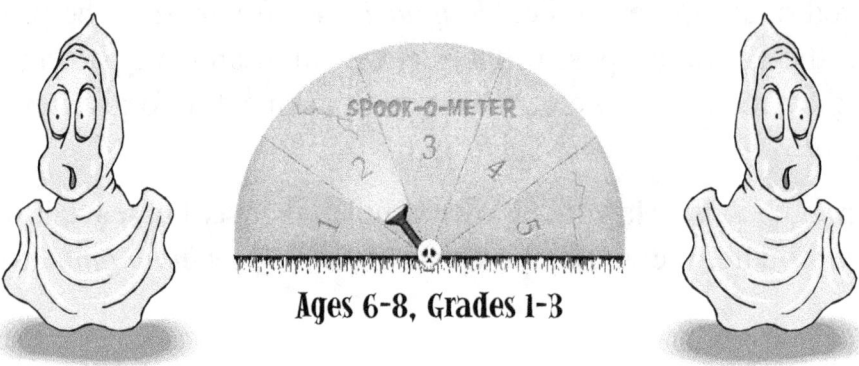

Ages 6-8, Grades 1-3

> *Note from Dianne:* "The Ghost of John" is a story that I cobbled together from a funny childhood playground song and a story summary told to me by a student at Haslet Elementary School in Haslet, Texas. This version is uproariously funny and I added a song at the end to maximize the humor of the story. It does rely on "bathroom" humor (pun intended) so be forewarned. It's a perfect spooktacular tale for a family, campfire, or anytime setting. You'll have a great time telling this tale!

There was once a family of five. [*Hold up one hand.*] There was Papa. [*Laugh deeply.*] There was Mama. [*Laugh in a high pitch voice.*] There was Brother. [*Flex muscles and pose in a "strong man" stance.*] There was Sister. [*Pat your hair in a prissy manner while wiggling your hips.*] And there was Baby Boo. [*Mime rocking a baby and suck on your thumb.*]

Now this family of five [*hold up one hand*] was on vacation in New Orleans. They were staying in an old Victorian mansion that was converted into a bed and breakfast. It was supposed to be . . . haunted! [*Pause and then emphasize the word "haunted."*] The townsfolk warned the family, "Don't stay in that mansion because it is haunted by the ghost of John."

But of course, the family paid them no mind. They said, "Everyone knows . . . [*pause*] there are no such thing as ghosts." [*Point index finger and wave finger from side to side, signifying "no."*] They brought their suitcases in anyway.

That night, Papa had to go to the bathroom. So he walked down the hall like this. [*Create a rhythm for each character walking down the hall.*]

He went inside the bathroom and dropped his drawers. Suddenly, he heard a spooky voice coming from the toilet!

The voice said:

"I see your hiney

"All big and shiny

You better hide it

Before I bite it!" [*Sing in a sing-song ghostly voice.*]

Papa pulled up his jammy pants and ran out of the bathroom, screaming down the hall back to the room. He said, "Mama, mama! There's a ghost in the toilet!

Mama laughed hysterically. [*High pitched laugh.*] "Papa, your imagination has gotten the best of you in this big spooky mansion. Now go back to sleep!"

Later that night, Mama had to go to the bathroom. So she walked down the hall like this. [*Create a rhythm for Mama walking down the hall.*]

She went inside the bathroom and dropped her drawers. Suddenly, she heard a spooky voice coming from the toilet!

The voice said:

"I see your hiney

"All big and shiny

You better hide it

Before I bite it!" [*Sing in a sing-song ghostly voice.*]

Mama pulled up her jammy pants and ran out of the bathroom, screaming down the hall back to the room. She said, "Papa, Papa! You're right. There's a ghost in the toilet!

Brother heard all the commotion and woke up. He laughed and said, "I think you guys are getting old. Besides, I'm strong. HUH! [*Flex arms like a strong man.*] and I'll protect you. Now go back to sleep!"

Later that night, Brother had to go to the bathroom. So he walked down the hall like this. [*Create a rhythm for Brother walking down the hall.*]

He went inside the bathroom and dropped his drawers. Suddenly, he heard a spooky voice coming from the toilet!

The voice said:

"I see your hiney

"All big and shiny

You better hide it

Before I bite it!" [*Sing in a sing-song ghostly voice.*]

Brother pulled up his jammy pants and ran out of the bathroom, screaming down the hall back to the room. He said, "Mama, Papa! You're right. There's a ghost in the toilet!

Sister heard all the commotion and woke up. She laughed and said, "I think you guys are going crazy. [*Rotate your pointer finger in a circular motion by your ear.*] Besides, I'm so cute, no ghost would dare touch me! [*Hold up an imaginary cell phone like you are taking a selfie.*] Now go back to sleep!"

Later that night, Sister had to go to the bathroom. So she walked down the hall like this. [*Create a rhythm for Sister walking down the hall.*]

She went inside the bathroom and dropped her drawers. Suddenly, she heard a spooky voice coming from the toilet!

The voice said:

"I see your hiney

"All big and shiny

You better hide it

Before I bite it!" [*Sing in a sing-song ghostly voice.*]

Sister pulled up her jammy pants and ran out of the bathroom, screaming down the hall back to the room. She said, "Mama, Papa, Brother! You're right. There's a ghost in the toilet!

While the four of them huddled together in fear under the covers, Baby Boo laughed. [*Suck your thumb and laugh like a baby.*] "I'm not afraid of no ghost 'cause a baby's gotta do what a baby's gotta do!" [*Say in a very funny baby voice.*]

So Baby Boo walked to the bathroom down the hall like this. [*Create a rhythm for Baby Boo walking down the hall.*]

He went inside the bathroom and looked around. He sucked his thumb. "Mmmmmmm," he said pulling out this thumb, "I like it." [*Say in a very baby voice pronouncing "like" as "yike." Then put your thumb back in your mouth.*] Suddenly, he heard a spooky voice coming from the toilet!

The voice said:

"I see your hiney

"All big and shiny

You better hide it

Before I bite it!" [*Sing in a sing-song ghostly voice.*]

Baby Boo looked inside the toilet and said:

"Oh yeah?!!!

I see your body

Inside the potty

You better hush it

Before I flush it!"

Then Baby Boo reached over and flushed the toilet [*Make a toilet flushing sound like WHOOSH!*] and the ghost was sucked down the whirlpool of water, never to be seen again. The Ghost of John was a gone pecan! No one before had ever thought to simply flush the toilet! The moral of this story is "Always flush and never leave anything BEHIND." [*Emphasize "behind" and wiggle your hiney from side to side.*]

The Ghost with One Black Eye

Ages 6-8, Grades 1-3

Note from Dianne: "The Ghost with One Black Eye" is a classic shaggy dog campfire ghost story. It is much like the story of "The Ghost of John" with a punch line at the end. This is a great story to tell in a family setting or with a mixed-age group of kids.

My granddaddy used to run a hotel that everyone said was haunted. In fact, my granddaddy said it was haunted too, by the ghost with . . . One. Black. Eye. [*Pause dramatically after "ghost with" and emphasize each word of "One" "Black" "Eye."*] A loooong time ago, [*Draw out the word "long."*] waaaaay [*Draw out the word "way."*] before you were born, a tough cowboy got into a fight. He got punch in the eye and his whole eye turned black. He died in the room he rented and my granddaddy insisted that the room was haunted. He used to tell me the story like this . . . [*Trail off and change your voice to be "granddaddy."*]

One day, I was sitting at the counter when a BIG rodeo cowboy [*Motion with your arms that the cowboy was BIG*] came in. He said, "I need a room."

I said to him, "Well, I only have one room left and I can't rent it to you because it's haunted by the ghost with . . . One. Black. Eye. [*Pause dramatically after "ghost with" and emphasize each word of "One" "Black" "Eye."*]

Well that BIG rodeo cowboy [*Motion with your arms that the cowboy was BIG.*] said, "I ain't afraid of no bulls and I ain't afraid of no ghosts. Give me the room."

What was I to do? I gave him the key and we went to the room. While he was in the room, that BIG rodeo cowboy [*Motion with your arms that the cowboy was BIG*] heard a ghostly voice cry out, "I'm the ghost with one black eye. I'm coming for you, big rodeo guy." [*Say this in a very lilting, ghostly voice.*]

That BIG rodeo cowboy [*Motion with your arms that the cowboy was BIG.*] ran out of the room, never to be seen again. [*Scream and motion exaggerated running.*]

Word got around and I didn't have to worry about renting the room until a couple of years later. I was sitting at the counter when a BAD outlaw [*Make a mean face.*] came in. He said, "I need a room."

I said to him, "Well, I only have one room left and I can't rent it to you because it's haunted by the ghost with . . . One. Black. Eye. [*Pause dramatically after "ghost with" and emphasize each word of "One" "Black" "Eye."*]

Well that BAD outlaw [*Make a mean face.*] said, "I ain't afraid of the law and I ain't afraid of no ghosts. Give me the room."

How could I argue? I gave him the key and he went to the room. While he was in the room, that BAD outlaw [*Make a mean face.*] heard a ghostly voice cry out, "I'm the ghost with one black eye. I'm coming for you, tough outlaw guy." [*Say this in a very lilting, ghostly voice, raising your voice slightly more than the last time you said it.*]

That that BAD outlaw [*Make a mean face.*] ran out of the room, never to be seen again. [*Scream and motion exaggerated running.*]

Well, it was a few more years before I had someone ask for that room again. One day, I was sitting at the counter when a TOUGH sheriff [*Flex your arms to mime strength.*] came in. He said, "I need a room."

I said to him, "Well, I only have one room left and I can't rent it to you because it's

haunted by the ghost with . . . One. Black. Eye. [*Pause dramatically after "ghost with" and emphasize each word of "One" "Black" "Eye."*]

Well that TOUGH sheriff [*Flex your arms to mime strength.*] said, "I ain't afraid of no outlaws and I ain't afraid of no ghosts. Give me the room."

What could I do? He was the law. I gave him the key and he went to the room. While he was in the room, that TOUGH sheriff [*Flex your arms to mime strength.*] heard a ghostly voice cry out, "I'm the ghost with one black eye. I'm coming for you, tough sheriff guy." [*Say this in a very lilting, ghostly voice, raising your voice slightly more than the last time you said it.*]

That TOUGH sheriff [*Flex your arms to mime strength.*] ran out of the room, never to be seen again. [*Scream and motion exaggerated running.*]

A good fifty years passed and I had all but forgotten about that room. One day, I was sitting at the counter when a sweet mom and her BRATTY little boy [*Stick out your tongue and blow a raspberry.*] came in. She said, "I need a room."

I said to her, "Well, I only have one room left and I can't rent it to you because it's haunted by the ghost with . . . One. Black. Eye. [*Pause dramatically after "ghost with" and emphasize each word of "One" "Black" "Eye."*]

Well that BRATTY little boy [*Stick out your tongue and blow a raspberry.*] said, "I ain't afraid of no bullies and I ain't afraid of no ghosts. Give us the room."

I shrugged my shoulders. He was the boss. I gave them the key and they went to the room. While they were in the room getting ready for bed, that BRATTY little boy [*Stick out your tongue and blow a raspberry.*] heard a ghostly voice cry out, "I'm the ghost with one black eye. I'm coming for you, bratty little guy." [*Say this in a very lilting, ghostly voice, raising your voice slightly more than the last time you said it.*]

That BRATTY little boy [*Stick out your tongue and blow a raspberry.*] looked at the ghost with . . . One. Black. Eye. [*Pause dramatically after "ghost with" and emphasize each word of "One" "Black" "Eye."*] and said, "If you don't be quiet, you'll be the ghost with TWO. BLACK. EYES. [*Emphasize each word of "Two" "Black" "Eyes."*] Then the BRATTY little boy stuck out his tongue and blew a big . . . RASPBERRY. [*Stick out your tongue and blow a raspberry. Encourage the audience to do it with you.*]

Optional Ending:

[*Switch to narrator voice.*] The ghost with . . . One. Black. Eye. [*Pause dramatically after "ghost with" and emphasize each word of "One" "Black" "Eye."*] was never seen again. At least that's the story my granddaddy told me!

Ginny Greenteeth

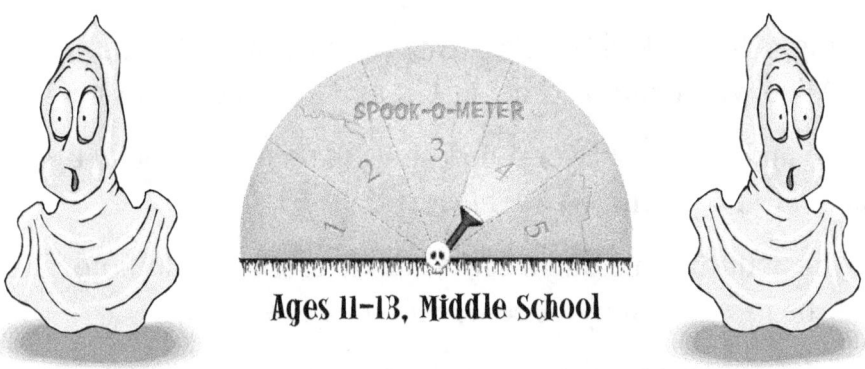

Ages 11-13, Middle School

Note from Dianne: This is an old English folktale that was told much like the bogey man, to keep children in check. Sometimes, she was used to threaten children if they didn't clean their teeth but mostly she was used as a way to keep children from water ways. I've rated it a solid 4 but depending on how you tell it, it could go up to a 5 because it involves the drowning of a child.

[*Begin story by saying this rhyme in a somber chant.*]

Children, children, you must beware.

Listen closely or be in for a scare.

Whatever you do, you must behave

Or Ginny Green Teeth takes you to your grave.

Ginny Green Teeth is a watery witch that lives at the bottom of the lake. She has pale green skin, sharp green teeth, long bony fingers with talon-like nails, [*Wiggle your fingers in front of you to signify bony fingers.*] and long locks of dark stringy hair. She seems to know when children misbehave and she always waits for them just beyond the water's edge.

In the morning, Alice gave her mother a hard time when her mother woke her up for school. She screamed, "I don't want to get up." [*Say this with a big, whiny attitude.*]

Her mother said, "Alice, you better be nice or Ginny Greenteeth will get you!"

Alice laughed and replied, "Everyone knows that is just a made up story. There's . . . no such thing as . . . [*pause*] Ginny Greenteeth!"

So Alice went to school and the day began like any other day. She stole lunch money from the little kids, she never turned in her homework, and she gave her teachers ATTITUDE. [*Snap your fingers in a "Z" formation with attitude!*] She was so mischievous and so bad that everyone nick-named her "Malice."

In the morning, Alice talked back to the teacher during a lesson. The teacher scolded Alice and said, "Alice, you better be nice or Ginny Greenteeth will get you!"

Alice laughed and replied, "Everyone knows that is just a made up story. There's . . . no such thing as . . . [*pause*] Ginny Greenteeth!"

At lunch, Alice cut the line and stole a cookie from a little boy. The little boy said, "Alice, you better be nice or Ginny Greenteeth will get you!"

Alice laughed and replied, "Everyone knows that is just a made up story. There's . . . no such thing as . . . [*Pause and allow audience to chime in.*] Ginny Greenteeth!"

On the playground, she pushed a little girl out of the way so she could ride the swing. The little girl said, "Alice, you better be nice or Ginny Greenteeth will get you!"

Alice laughed and replied, "Everyone knows that is just a made up story. There's . . . no such thing as . . . [*Pause and allow audience to chime in.*] Ginny Greenteeth!"

That day, Alice made everyone mad because she was bad, bad, bad. On the way home from school, Alice decided to take the road her mother told her to never take. The road that led to the . . . [*pause*] lake!

Alice approached the water and looked in. She said, There's . . . no such thing as . . . [*Pause and allow audience to chime in.*] Ginny Greenteeth!"

Suddenly . . . [*pause*] a woman with a pale green skin, sharp green teeth, long bony fingers with talon-like nails, [*Wiggle your fingers in front of you to signify bony fingers.*] and long locks of dark, stringy hair [*Say this loudly.*] LUNGED out of the water. She grabbed Alice and clutched her tight, dragging her into the murky water of the lake, down, down, down to her watery grave.

A few days later, after an extensive search, Alice was found near the bottom of the lake She was wrapped in what at first looked like water weeds. But upon closer inspection, the police discovered that Alice was covered in long locks of dark, stringy hair! [*Mime playing with long hair.*]

    Children, children, you must beware.

    Listen closely or be in for a scare.

    Whatever you do, you must behave

    Or Ginny Green Teeth takes you to your grave.

The Graveyard Bone

Ages 6-8, Grades 1-3

Note from Dianne: "The Graveyard Bone" is a loosely adapted American version of "The Big Hairy Toe" and "Taily Po." It is a classic jump story. It makes a great campfire, slumber, rainy day, or any day story. Although the title is ominous, the story is actually humorous and is great for younger audiences. You can really ham it up until the final moments when you execute the "Gotcha!" jump.

There was once an old woman who was on her way home from the market. She cut through the graveyard and found a bone sticking out of the grass. She didn't know it, but it was a funny bone. She gave it a great big jerk and pulled it out of the ground. The old woman took the graveyard bone home and she [*pause*] made a soup with it! Then she set the table and she [*pause*] ATE it! [*Be prepared for a lot of "ewwwws" and/or laughter from your audience.*]

It sure was tasty. Yum! Yum! Yum! [*Rub belly with each "Yum!"*] Then the woman went to bed.

Outside, the wind picked up and howled.

Hoooooooooooooooooooooooooooooo

Hoooooooooooooooooooooooooooooo

[*Invite audience to join in the howling wind.*]

Then, in the distance, a voice cried out,

"I won't go home! I won't go home!

Until you give back my funny bone!"

[*Say this soft and draw out the long vowel "O" in each "bone."*]

The woman buried herself under her blanket and said, with her ears in her fingers:

"La! La! La! La! La! La!"

"La! La! La! La! La! La!"

[*Do this part very comically. The woman is trying to drown out the sound.*]

Outside, the rain began to fall. [*Clap hands softly against thighs and invite audience to join in.*] And the wind continued to howl.

Hooooooooooooooooooooooooooooo

Hooooooooooooooooooooooooooooo

Then, closer than before, a voice cried out,

"I won't go home! I won't go home!

Until you give back my funny bone!"

[*Say this soft and draw out the long vowel "O" in each "bone."*]

The woman buried herself even deeper under her blanket and said, with her ears in her fingers:

"La! La! La! La! La! La!"

"La! La! La! La! La! La!"

[*Do this part even more exaggerated.*]

Outside, the thunder roared. BOOM! [*Clap hands simultaneously while yelling "BOOM!" and repeat. The audience will join in.*] The rain fell. [*Clap hands softly against thighs.*] And the wind continued to howl.

Hooooooooooooooooooooooooooooo

Hooooooooooooooooooooooooooooo

Then all was ssshhhh . . . [*pause*] silent. [*Pause for three seconds of silence, cupping ear with hand to listen.*] Inside the house, right next to her [*pause*] BED a voice cried out,

"I won't go home! I won't go home!

Until you give back my funny bone!"

[*Say this VERY LOUD and draw out the long vowel "O" in each "bone."*]

[*Say this next part quietly but excitedly.*] The woman jumped out of bed and ran into the kitchen. She reached into the pot, threw the bone out of the window, and said,

"TAKE IT!" [*Yell out the last two words, causing the audience to jump.*]

The Hairdo

Ages 11-13, Middle School

> *Note from Dianne:* "The Hairdo" is retelling of a popular urban legend. It has the creepy factor because it has spiders in the story. I've amped up the comedy of this outrageous urban legend but it has a (warning) gross ending so tell the story at your discretion. And wash your hair. No really.

Sally loved all the latest fads. She loved clothes, she loved hair, and she loved makeup! [*Bat your eyelashes.*] Everyone called Sally a beauty queen. [*Pat your hair like you are a "beauty queen."*] Everyone called Sally a fashionista. [*Prance like you are on a fashion runway.*] Everyone called Sally a . . . [*pause dramatically*] diva. [*Snap your fingers in the air in a "Z" formation with a little "attitude."*]

Believe it or not, beehive bouffant hairdos were all the rage! [*Punctuate the words "all the rage."*] The bigger, the better. The higher, the happier. The tallest, the best! [*Place hand above head and raise hand higher and higher with each superlative.*] So of course, Sally had to have the biggest, the highest, and the tallest beehive bouffant hairdo in her entire town. Why, her reputation depended upon it!

Sally went to her local beauty salon and said, "Beatrice," I need the biggest, the highest, and the tallest beehive bouffant hairdo ever." [*Place hand above head and raise hand higher and higher with each superlative.*]

Beatrice was happy to comply with Sally's request. She combed, and teased, and sprayed until that beehive bouffant hairdo was nearly as tall as the ceiling! People in the shop gathered around to admire Sally. The townsfolk stopped in front of the beauty shop to gaze in the window. Sally definitely had the biggest, the highest, and the tallest beehive bouffant hairdo *ever*." [*Place hand above head and raise hand higher and higher with each superlative. Emphasize "ever" with attitude.*]

Sally walked out of the shop feeling like a beauty queen [*Pat your hair like you are a "beauty queen."*], a fashionista, [*Prance like you are on a fashion runway.*] and a . . . [*pause dramatically*] diva. [*Snap your fingers in the air in a "Z" formation with a little "attitude."*]

As she was walking home, she passed beneath a tree. Unbeknownst to Sally, a spider from the tree fell into her hair. For the next few weeks, Sally kept her beehive bouffant hairdo in tact. She covered it when she showered, she wrapped it when she slept, and she protected it from all the elements. [*Mime protecting hair.*] She never brushed her hair out. Her fashionable hair had to be absolute perfection!

One day, Sally was in class when she noticed blood dripping down her forehead. It was coming from her scalp. She fainted and she was rushed to the hospital. At the hospital, Sally was pronounced DOA—dead on arrival. When the doctors examined her head, a nest of spiders burst out of her beehive bouffant hairdo by the thousands. And all those spiders had . . . [*pause dramatically*] EATEN HER BRAIN. [*Make a comically gruesome face.*]

The Hook

> *Note from Dianne:* "The Hook" is an urban legend that has many versions. It relies on our fear of criminals, the dark, and the unknown. It has some mature content so I have rated this one a 5 on the Spook-O-Meter.

Bobby drove off the main road into a wooded area so that he and Janet could have some alone time. He parked the car under a tree. He put on some music, just to create some background noise. [*Bop head to an imaginary beat.*]

Just as Bobby put his arm around his girlfriend, the radio blared: [*Tell in a louder than normal voice.*]:

"We interrupt this program to bring you breaking news. A serial killer has escaped the local insane asylum and he is on the loose. He can be identified by the hook on his arm that replaces his left hand. He is dangerous and, as a precaution, everyone should stay inside."

The music returned and Bobby glanced at Janet, who looked like she had seen a ghost. [*Look scared.*]

"What's the matter, Janet?" Bobby asked.

Janet stuttered, "Don't, don't you think we should get out of here? I'm scared." [*Stutter and act nervous.*]

Bobby answered, "Nah! What are the chances a serial killer is in this same exact spot as us, right here, right now?!"

Still, Janet was insistent. "I mean it, Bobby. I want to go HOME." [*Raise voice slightly when saying "home."*]

"Fine." It was clear that Bobby was pretty mad. He peeled out and sped out of the forest onto the highway. When they reached Janet's house, he got out of the car to open the door for her and he couldn't believe what he saw . . .

[*SCREAM!*]

A bloody metal hook, which had been attached to someone's arm was hanging off the door handle . . . [*Let your voice trail off.*]

I'm Coming for Your Soul!

Ages 9–10, Grades 4–5

Note from Dianne: "I'm Coming for Your Soul" is a completely original story. I love puns and I wrote this story in the tradition of the shaggy dog tale. It can be embellished, with the suspense and tension drawn out. It's a great story for elementary-aged audiences, who will get the joke at the end of the tale.

Jack was a naughty little boy. He got into all kinds of mischief and wouldn't listen to his mom. [*Say "hmph" and put your hands on your hips.*] She told him that if he didn't behave, the oogie woogie boogie man [*Emphasize "oogie woogie boogie man" and say it in a slightly spooky voice.*] would come and get him. Still, Jack wouldn't listen to his mom so she sent him to bed without any supper.

Jack went to his room and changed into his jammies. He lay in his bed and began reading his favorite book. It was a nice night so his window was open. That's when he heard a ghostly voice . . .

"I'm coming for your soul, I'm coming for your soul!" [*Say this is a lilting, ghostly voice and draw out the sound in the word "soul."*]

Jack thought perhaps he was hearing things but he got under the covers anyway. He shook it off and began reading his book again. The curtain in the window began to blow. Jack heard that ghostly voice again . . .

"I'm coming for your soul, I'm coming for your soul!" [*Say this is a lilting, ghostly voice and draw out the sound in the word "soul." Raise your voice.*]

Now Jack was truly nervous. Maybe his mom was right! Maybe the oogie woogie boogie man [*Emphasize "oogie woogie boogie man" and say it in a slightly spooky voice.*] was coming for him! Jack pulled the covers up to his chest. Nothing. So again, he shook it off and began reading his book. The curtain in the window began to blow. The dresser in his room began to shake. Jack heard that ghostly voice again . . .

"I'm coming for your soul, I'm coming for your soul!" [*Say this is a lilting, ghostly voice and draw out the sound in the word "soul." Raise your voice.*]

Jack put the book down. He pulled the covers over his head, afraid to look at the window. He began thinking how sorry he was for all the mischievous things he did and how sorry he was that he didn't listen to his mom. Jack peeked out of the covers.

The curtain in the window began to blow. The dresser in his room began to shake. The television turned on by itself! Jack heard that ghostly voice again . . .

"I'm coming for your soul, I'm coming for your soul!" [*Say this is a lilting, ghostly voice and draw out the sound in the word "soul." Raise your voice.*]

Jack was terrified but he couldn't stand it anymore. He yelled, "Fine! Take it!" Jack threw his shoe at the window and it disappeared. [*Mime throwing a shoe.*]

A moment later the oogie woogie boogie man appeared in the window and said, "Thanks! I needed a new sole. A SHOE SOLE."

Irish Eyes

Note from Dianne: "Irish Eyes" is an original story. I had a doll collection when I was growing up and she was part of my collection. There are many stories of cursed dolls. It is a popular motif that can even be seen in the movies like *Chucky* and *Annabelle*. Dolls scare me and they scare lots of children so proceed with caution when telling this tale . . .

I was so excited to receive the box my father gave me. A friend of his had been traveling in Ireland and brought this special gift back for me.

"Open it," my father urged.

I ripped the brown paper off the box. [*Mime ripping paper off a box.*] There, inside the box, under a cellophane window, was a doll in a white and green shamrock dress. She had fiery red hair and the most penetrating blue eyes I had ever seen. Immediately, the hairs on the back of my neck stood up and I caught the chills. Had I known then what I know now, I would have NEVER opened the box! [*Emphasize "never."*]

"She's for your collection. What do you think?" my father implored.

"Um . . . [*pause*] She's pretty."

Well, she was pretty but truthfully, there was something about her I didn't like right away. My father told me to bring the new doll upstairs and store the box in my closet. I did as I was told. My hutch was filled with dolls from all over the world. My father traveled and so did his friends. Everywhere my dad and his friends traveled for work, they brought me back a doll. I had dolls from Korea, Japan, the Philippines, Spain, and Hawaii. I loved my dolls. That is, until Irish Eyes came along . . . [*Lower voice and speak ominously, then pause.*]

I placed the doll on the top shelf, in the very back. [*Mime placing the doll on the shelf.*] I shoved her behind all the other dolls so that I wouldn't have to look at her terrifying icy blue eyes and scarlet lips. I felt like the doll was watching me.

The next morning, I woke up just before dawn. [*Yawn and stretch.*] I never woke up that early but I slept fitfully and had bad dreams. Out of habit, I looked up at my doll hutch. All the dolls were pushed over. Some of the dolls were on the floor. Irish Eyes was the only doll standing, and she was standing right in the front. I screamed. [*Scream.*]

My mother came running into my room, "What's wrong?

I pointed to the dolls. My mother frowned but didn't say anything. Silently, she began picking up the dolls and placing them on the hutch. She didn't even ask me what happened. But I knew she knew too.

Later that day, I decided to take matters into my own hands. I grabbed the box from the closet and took Irish Eyes off the shelf. She was half smiling or was she smirking? I shoved her in the box and wrapped the box with masking tape. [*Mime putting the doll in the box and wrapping the box with tape.*] I stuck the box deep into the rear of my closet, underneath a pile of junk. There. I wouldn't have to see her again. I was wrong.

The next day, when I woke up, Irish Eyes was . . . [*pause*] on the foot of my bed! Just standing there, staring me at. All the other dolls were on the floor. The box was in the middle of the floor, the masking tape ripped apart. "Father!" I screamed.

My father came running in and stared at my room. "Is this your idea of a joke?" he asked. "It's not very funny." [*Use a deep voice.*]

I was so shaken I couldn't respond. He ordered me to pick up my dolls and clean my room. It seemed as though Irish Eyes was sneering at me. I swear, I saw evil behind those lifeless, jarring blue eyes.

I took the wicked doll and shoved her back inside the box. This time, I wrapped so much tape around the box that there was no possible way she could get out. [*Mime vehemently putting the doll in the box and wrapping the box with tape.*] I brought her outside to the curbside garbage. I shoved her deep inside the can, and covered her up with tons of trash. She was never going to bother me again. [*Mime shoving doll in the garbage can.*]

That night, I tossed and turned and had nightmares. The evil doll was taunting me, laughing in my face. I woke up, sweating. I turned on my light. It was just a nightmare. Then I looked down. The doll was IN MY BED! [*Say this with horror.*] She was smiling. I heard a giggle.

I screamed and began rocking back and forth. [*Rock back and forth.*] I couldn't stand her. I had to get away from that horrid doll. Crying hysterically, I ran out of my room and out of the house barefoot and in my pajamas. [*Mime running away.*] My parents woke up and my father began chasing me. He caught me halfway down and street and tried to console me as my body shook with heaving sobs. My parents took me to the doctor and the doctor suggested that I be committed to a residential hospital. In heated whispers and hushed tones, my parents discussed my fate with the doctor. I didn't care as long as I could get away from her . . .

They put me in a padded cell just for "observation." Finally, I was free from that wretched doll. My mother and father came to say goodbye and to tell me that they would be visiting soon. Mother hugged me and left the room. Father came to say goodbye and pulled something out of his jacket. He placed a small paper bag on the bed. [*Mime placing a bag on the bed.*]

"For you, sweetheart. Your favorite." Father left.

I opened the bag slowly . . . [*pause*] AND THERE SHE WAS! [*Raise your voice saying "And there she was!"*] She mocked me. She tortured me with her evil smile. I heard her wicked giggle in my head. I started screaming but no one could hear me. Nobody came. I was alone with . . . [*pause*]

Irish Eyes . . . [*Let your voice trail off.*]

It Floats!

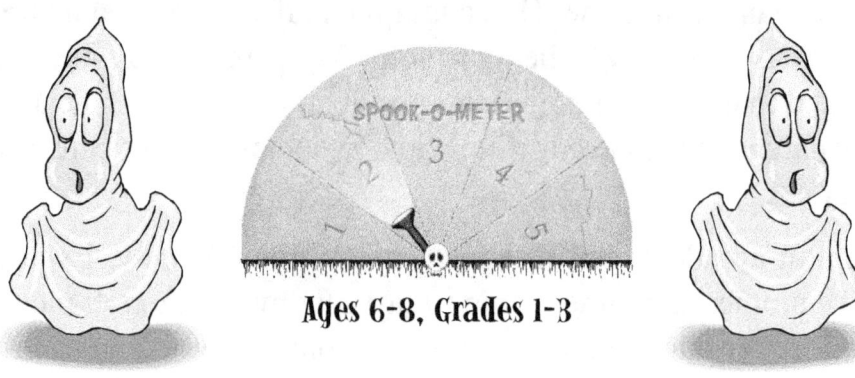

Ages 6-8, Grades 1-3

> *Note from Dianne:* This is a great story to do with younger kids. To "de-scarify" the story, I have them participate in the story with me by chanting "It flooooats! It flooooats!" Even if you don't prompt them to participate, they will naturally do so. It is a shaggy dog tale with a big joke at the end, which helps to relieve any tension.

It was summer and the Millers were going on vacation. Kevin packed up the car and Angel finally got their two boys, Casey and Cody, settled in the back seat.

"Are we ready to go?" yelled Kevin.

The two boys yelled YES! [*Yell "yes!"*] and started singing, "We're going on vacation. We're going on vacation!" [*Sing this in a childish voice.*]

Angel sighed. "I can see this is going to be a long ride. Did you decide where we're going yet, Kevin?"

Kevin said, "Nah. We're going on the road less traveled to have an adventure. Am I right, boys?"

The two boys yelled YES! [*Yell "yes!"*] and started singing, "We're going on an adventure. We're going on an adventure!" [*Sing this in a childish voice.*]

About five hours into the drive, Angel woke up from dozing off. She didn't recognize where they were. The boys were sleeping in the back seat [*Snore.*] and Kevin was tapping the steering wheel to the beat of an 80s hair band song.

He sang, "You give love a bad name!" [*Sing this part.*]

"Very funny," said Angel. Where are we?"

Kevin answered, "Beats me. I turned off the main road so we could explore the country side."

Angel said, "You what?" She looked at her cell phone but there was no service. What could she do? Her husband had a mind of his own.

They rounded a bend and Kevin spotted an old motel. "This looks great!" he said. "We are going to stay here tonight!"

The Millers settled into a room with two queen beds. Kevin looked at Angel, "See? It's not that bad . . ."

Angel snorted, "Hmph."

Cody said, "Mom, I have to go to the potty!" [*Say this in a whiney kid voice.*]

Angel answered, "Go ahead, honey. You're a big boy. You know where it is."

Cody went into the bathroom and heard a disembodied voice cry out, "It flooooats! It flooooats!" [*Say this in a lilting ghostly voice, drawing out the "O" sound in "float."*]

Cody ran out of the room, screaming, "Mom, Dad, there's a ghost in the bathroom saying 'It floats! It floats!'"

Kevin said, "Buddy. Ghosts are made up. Go to bed." He patted Cody on the head and tucked him in. [*Pat a child on the head.*]

Later, Casey had to use the potty. He went into the bathroom and heard a disembodied voice cry out, "It flooooats! It flooooats!" [*Say this in a lilting ghostly voice, drawing out the "O" sound in "float."*]

Casey ran out of the room, screaming, "Mom, Dad, there's a ghost in the bathroom saying 'It floats! It floats!'"

Kevin said, "Buddy. Ghosts are . . . [*Pause and let audience chime in.*] made up. Go to bed." He patted Casey on the head and tucked him in. [*Pat a child on the head.*]

Later, Kevin had to use the potty. He went into the bathroom and heard a disembodied voice cry out, "It flooooats! It flooooats!" [*Say this in a lilting ghostly voice, drawing out the "O" sound in "float."*]

Kevin ran out of the room, screaming, "Angel, there's a ghost in the bathroom saying 'It floats! It floats!'"

Angel said, "REALLY, Kevin?! You're just like a little kid. Stay here." [*Act like an annoyed mom.*]

Angel went into the bathroom and looked around. Soon, she heard a disembodied voice cry out, "It flooooats! It flooooats!" [*Say this in a lilting ghostly voice, drawing out the "O" sound in "float."*]

Angel placed her hand on her hips and asked, annoyed, "WHAT FLOATS?" [*Place hands on hips and say this in an annoyed voice.*]

"Ivory Soap! Ivory Soap flooooats!"

Angel looked into the tub and sure enough, she saw a floating bar of . . . [*pause*] Ivory Soap.

La Llorona (The Wailing Woman)

Note from Dianne: "La Llorona" is a Mexican/Mexican American ghost tale that has no discernible origin. Over the years, I have heard many versions of the story from other storytellers, especially in Texas. It's a classic ghost tale but can be particularly chilling because it involves a mother killing her children. This is my version. Tell it with discretion.

Dolores came from a poor family. Her husband had passed away a few years before and she struggled to put food on the table for her and her two children.

One day, she went to the market and a wealthy Ranchero began flirting with her. She was overwhelmed and flattered but thought nothing of it when she went home.

For next few weeks, every time she went to the market, she saw the Ranchero and he made his intentions clear. He asked if he could see her at his ranch. Of course, Dolores said, "Yes!" [*Say "yes" enthusiastically.*] There was only one caveat. [*Pause dramatically.*] Dolores had to enter through the back door, where the servants entered. Although she thought this was odd, she complied with his request, happy to have a companion in her life again.

The Ranchero and Dolores saw each other often. She always entered his home through the rear door, never questioning the reason. She was just happy to be with him. [*Sigh like you are "in love."*]

One day, Dolores and her Ranchero were having a romantic lunch on his veranda when he blurted out, "I love you!" [*Say "I love you" with feeling.*]

Dolores was delighted. She responded, "I love you too!" She jumped up and hugged the Ranchero. [*Motion hugging or hug someone in the audience.*] Then Dolores said, "We should get married!" [*Say this excitedly.*]

The Ranchero did not know what to say. Although he cared deeply for Dolores, he knew he could not marry her. She came from a poor family. He was a wealthy Ranchero and could not have a peasant for his wife! [*Be indignant.*]

Although he did not mind that she had children from her previous marriage, he used it as an excuse to get out of marrying Dolores. He didn't want to tell her the truth. [*Lower voice when saying the following.*] He said, "Dolores, I am sorry but I cannot marry you because you have children from another man."

[*The tone of the story gets very dark here.*] Dolores was upset. She ran out of the house, crying. Her only chance at happiness was destroyed because of those two little beasts at home! She marched into the house and coaxed the children to come to the river with her.

Dolores pretended to go swimming with her children but instead, she drowned them, holding their heads under water until the river became their watery grave. She let them go and got out of the river.

Half-crazed and dripping wet, she ran all way the to the Ranchero's house, yelling, "They're gone. They're gone. Now we can be married!" [*Tell this in a voice with heightened excitement.*]

The Ranchero grabbed Dolores and asked, "What do you mean, 'They're gone?' Where did they go? Dolores, what happened to the children?" [*Ask this in a nervous and scared voice.*]

Dolores began laughing hysterically. "They are at the bottom of the river. I drowned them. Now we can be together forever!" [*Tell this in a hysterical voice.*]

The Ranchero was horrified. He ordered his servants to apprehend Dolores but she struggled against them and escaped. Dolores ran back to the river. Back to where she murdered her own children. She realized what she had done. She screamed and cried and wailed. [*Cry dramatically but not in a humorous way.*]

Then she walked into the river and breathed it all in, allowing the cold water to fill her lungs, punishing herself for her terrible deed.

To this day, La Llorona wanders and searches for her children. She weeps and wails, and when she comes across any children, she takes them away, hoping that one day, she will be forgiven for her sins.

Over in the Graveyard

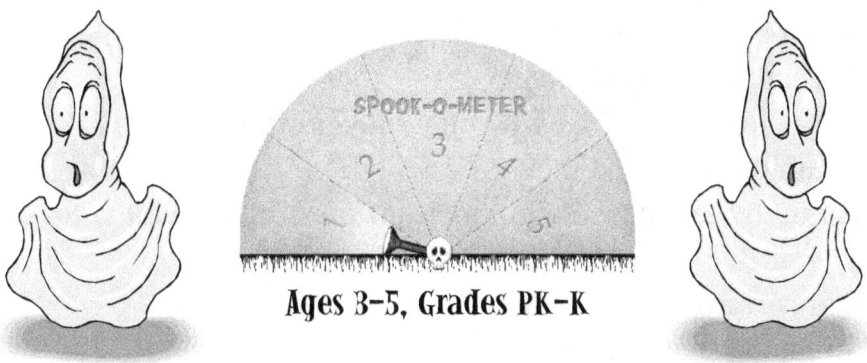

Ages 3-5, Grades PK-K

Note from Dianne: This is actually a song based on the traditional song, "Over in the Meadow." It's a great counting song and perfect for any Halloween programs designed for the little ones.

Over in the graveyard
On the tomb in the moon, lived an
Old mother spider and her
Little spider one. [*Hold up 1 finger.*]
"Spin," said the mother, [*Make a spinning motion with your hands.*]
"I spin," said the one, and they
Spun all night on the tomb in the moon. [*Make a spinning motion with your hands.*]

Over in the graveyard where the
Witches stir the brew, lived an
Old mother ghost and her
Little ghosties two. [*Hold up 2 fingers.*]
"Boo!," said the mother, [*Make a "boo!" gesture with your hands and face.*]
We "boo!," said the two, and they
Booed all night where the witches stir the brew. [*Make a "boo!" gesture with your hands and face.*]

Over in the graveyard on a branch on the tree,
Lived an old mother owl and her
Little owls three. [*Hold up 3 fingers.*]
"Hoot," said the mother, [*Cup hands by mouth.*]
"We hoot," said the three, and they
Hooted all night on a branch on the tree. [*Cup hands by mouth.*]

Over in the graveyard by the mausoleum door,
Lived an old mother cat and her
Little kitties four. [*Hold up 4 fingers.*]
"Mew," said the mother, [*Mime pawing with your hands.*]
"We mew," said the four, and they
Mewed all night by the mausoleum door. [*Mime pawing with your hands.*]

Over in the graveyard feeling quite alive,
Lived an old mother bat and her
Little batties five. [*Hold up 5 fingers.*]
"Flap," said the mother, [*Mime flapping with your arms.*]
"We flap," said the five, and they
Flapped all night feeling quite alive.

Over in the graveyard with the treats and the tricks,
Lived an old mother pumpkin and her
Little pumpkins six. [*Hold up 6 fingers.*]
"Roll," said the mother, [*Mime a rolling motion with your hands.*]
"We roll," said the six, and they
Rolled all night with the treats and the tricks. [*Mime a rolling motion with your hands.*]

Over in the graveyard underneath the heavens.
Lived old mother bones and her
Little skeletons seven. [*Hold up 7 fingers.*]
"Rattle," said the mother, [*Shake arms in front of you.*]
"We rattle," said the seven, and they
Rattled all night underneath the heavens. [*Shake arms in front of you.*]

Over in the graveyard by the old creaky gate,
Lived an old mother mummy and her
Little mummies eight. [*Hold up 8 fingers.*]
"Wrap," said the mother, [*Hug yourself.*]
"We wrap," said the eight, and they
Wrapped all night by the old creaky gate. [*Hug yourself.*]

Over in the graveyard by the long ivy vine,
Lived an old mother werewolf and her
Little werewolves nine. [*Hold up 9 fingers.*]
"Howl," said the mother, [*Tilt head back and mime howling life a wolf.*]
"We howl," said the nine, and they
Howled all night by the long ivy vine. [*Tilt head back and mime howling life a wolf.*]

Over in the graveyard in a mystical glen
Lived an old mother witch and her
Little witchies ten. [*Hold up all 10 fingers.*]
"Fly," said the mother, [*Wave one arm as if flying.*]
"We fly," said the ten, and they
Flew all night in a mystical glen. [*Wave one arm as if flying.*]

Pulling the Pumpkin

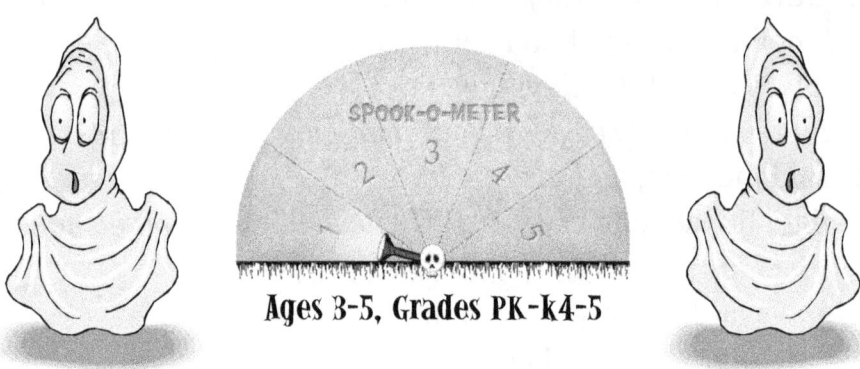

Ages 3-5, Grades PK-k4-5

> *Note from Dianne:* "Pulling the Pumpkin" is adapted from a Russian folktale called "The Enormous Turnip." I love this story because it lends itself to adaptations. I did a Louisiana version called *The Gigantic Sweet Potato*, which is a picture book. In this version, I twisted the tale for a Halloween version of the story. The characters are fun, and there is a lot of audience participation. It's perfect for young children.

Witchy planted a pumpkin. It grew and grew and grew until it was GIGANTIC. [*Spread arms wide to mime a gigantic pumpkin.*] It was ready to pull out of the patch. Witchy grabbed the pumpkin and she began to pull. [*Mime pulling and invite the audience to join in the story chorus.*]

She pulled and she pulled with a twist and a shout

But the pumpkin, pumpkin wouldn't come out

The pumpkin was stuck! Along came Frankenstein, who offered to help. Frankie grabbed Witchy. Witchy grabbed the pumpkin and they began to pull. [*Mime pulling and invite the audience to join in the story chorus.*]

They pulled and they pulled with a twist and a shout

But the pumpkin, pumpkin wouldn't come out

The pumpkin was still stuck. Along came Vampire, who offered to help. Vampy grabbed Frankie, Frankie grabbed Witchy, Witchy grabbed the pumpkin and they began to pull. [*Mime pulling and invite the audience to join in the story chorus.*]

They pulled and they pulled with a twist and a shout

But the pumpkin, pumpkin wouldn't come out

The pumpkin was still stuck. Along came Skeleton, who offered to help. Skelly grabbed Vampy, Vampy grabbed Frankie, Frankie grabbed Witchy, Witchy grabbed the pumpkin and they began to pull. [*Mime pulling and invite the audience to join in the story chorus.*]

They pulled and they pulled with a twist and a shout

But the pumpkin, pumpkin wouldn't come out

The pumpkin was still stuck! Along came Mummy, who offered to help. Mummy grabbed Skelly, Skelly grabbed Vampy, Vampy grabbed Frankie, Frankie grabbed Witchy, Witchy grabbed the pumpkin and they began to pull. [*Mime pulling and invite the audience to join in the story chorus.*]

They pulled and they pulled with a twist and a shout

But the pumpkin, pumpkin wouldn't come out

The pumpkin was still stuck! By this time, everyone was so tired that they wanted to give up. Along came Kitty, who offered to help. Witchy said, "You're too small. You can't help at all."

Kitty replied, "Let me show you what I'm about. With my help, we'll pull the pumpkin out." [*Point to yourself with your thumb and mime pulling the pumpkin.*]

So Witchy agreed. Kitty grabbed Mummy, Mummy grabbed Skelly, Skelly grabbed Vampy, Vampy grabbed Frankie, Frankie grabbed Witchy, Witchy grabbed the pumpkin and they began to pull. [*Mime pulling and invite the audience to join in the story chorus.*]

They pulled and they pulled with a twist and a shout

And the pumpkin, pumpkin—it came . . . out! [*Pause dramatically after "it came" and allow the audience to chime in "out."*]

Everyone cheered! [*Cheer and invite audience to cheer.*] With all that pumpkin, Witchy made a GIGANTIC pumpkin pie. [*Spread arms wide to mime a gigantic pumpkin pie.*] Vampire took the biggest bite. [*Mime taking a bite.*] Frankenstein cut his slice into pieces. Skeleton made his platter clatter. Mummy asked Witchy to wrap up his piece to go. But Kitty was such a gigantic help, she received the biggest piece. Kitty was, after all, the cat's meow!

And when everyone was done eating, guess what they did with the shell of that pumpkin? That's right! They all helped carve it into a grinning . . . JACK-O-LANTERN! [*Pause dramatically and then say "jack-o-lantern."*]

[*End the story with a repeat of the last story chorus.*]

They pulled and they pulled with a twist and a shout

And the pumpkin, pumpkin—it came out ! [*Pause dramatically after "it came" and allow the audience to chime in "out."*]

The Sack Filled with Treats

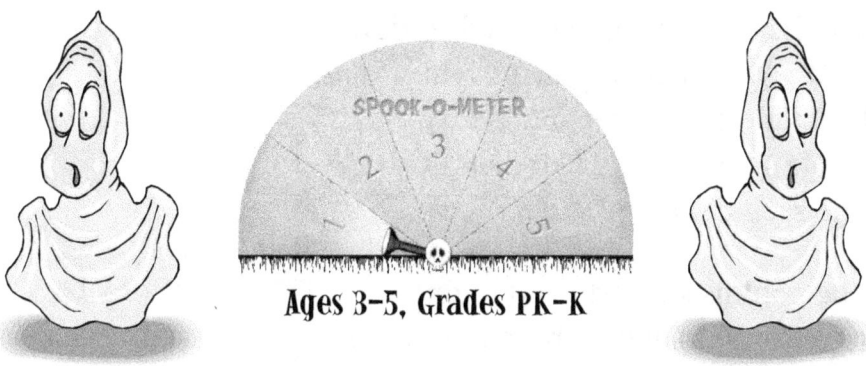

Ages 3-5, Grades PK-K

Note from Dianne: This original story is inspired by the structure of Mother Goose rhyme, "The House That Jack Built." There are many such stories that follow this rhyme scheme. It's cumulative and works with the very young.

This is the sack filled with treats

This is the cat, so big and black,
Who's sleeping soundly, just like that
On top of the sack filled with treats.

This is the mummy all wrapped so tight
Who jumps at you and gives you a fright
If you wake up the cat, so big and black,
Who's sleeping soundly, just like that
On top of the sack filled with treats.

This is the pumpkin, big and round
Who rolls his way up and down town
Right next to the mummy all wrapped so tight
Who jumps at you and gives you a fright

If you wake up the cat, so big and black,
Who's sleeping soundly, just like that
On top of the sack filled with treats.

This is the witch with sickly green skin
Who will cast a spell much to your chagrin
Beside the pumpkin, big and round
Who rolls his way up and down town
Right next to the mummy all wrapped so tight
Who jumps at you and gives you a fright
If you wake up the cat, so big and black,
Who's sleeping soundly, just like that
On top of the sack filled with treats.

These are the goblins so warty and plump
Who creep in the night and go bumpity-bump
Behind the witch with sickly green skin
Who will cast a spell much to your chagrin
Beside the pumpkin, big and round
Who rolls his way up and down town
Right next to the mummy all wrapped so tight
Who jumps at you and gives you a fright
If you wake up the cat, so big and black,
Who's sleeping soundly, just like that
On top of the sack filled with treats.

This is the vampire with long sharp fangs
Who gets all batty and likes to hang
Around the goblins so warty and plump
Who creep in the night and go bumpity-bump
Behind the witch with sickly green skin
Who will cast a spell much to your chagrin
Beside the pumpin, big and round
Who rolls his way up and down town
Right next to the mummy all wrapped so tight
Who jumps at you and gives you a fright
If you wake up the cat, so big and black,

Who's sleeping soundly, just like that
On top of the sack filled with treats.

This the spider who scared Vamp straight
Who ordered the goblins to go and skate
Who made the witch fly into the night
Who gave the pumpkin a nasty fright
Who unwrapped the mummy so he was free
Who woke up the cat so she could have tea
Who put on her headphones and listened to beats
And crawled inside the sack filled with treats.

Sneakers

Ages 9-10, Grades 4-5

> *Note from Dianne:* This is a story that is very hard to trace. I've heard many versions of it over the years but this is my favorite and I tweaked the ending a bit. It's a shaggy dog tale with a funny ending but it can really be "spookified" using anticipation and tension as the boy races through the forest.

Adam stayed out way too late. The sun was setting and it was getting dark quickly. Where did the time go? He had wandered through the forest near his home because, during the day, it wasn't all that spooky. But now that twilight was upon him, Adam saw shadows and heard things . . . [*pause*] He had to get home soon!

He began walking through the forest when he heard a distinct sound. Each time he stepped, he heard something step behind him.

STEP, DRAG . . .

STEP, DRAG . . . [*Use a deep, ominous voice.*]

When he looked back, there was nothing there. [*Mime looking behind you nervously.*]

Adam wished he hadn't wandered off so far. He wished that he had listened to his mom and stayed close to the house. Now, the sun had set and the forest was really dark. The only comforting thing for Adam was that he knew his way home on this particular trail.

Adam picked up the pace and walked faster. Again, each time he stepped, he heard something behind him.

STEP, DRAG . . .

STEP, DRAG . . . [*Use a deep, ominous voice.*]

When he looked back, there was nothing there. [*Mime looking behind you nervously.*]

Now Adam was terrified. He began running through the forest. He told himself that he would never again disobey his mother. If only he was home right now . . . he'd be in the comfort and safety of his own house. Of course, each time he stepped, he heard something behind him.

STEP, DRAG . . .

STEP, DRAG . . . [*Use a deep, ominous voice.*]

When he looked back, there was nothing there. [*Mime looking behind you nervously.*]

He ran faster and faster but no matter how quickly he made his way through the forest, it was always right there. Each time he stepped, he heard it behind him.

STEP, DRAG . . .

STEP, DRAG . . . [*Use a deep, ominous voice.*]

When he looked back, there was nothing there. [*Mime looking behind you nervously.*]

Adam just knew that something was going to SNEAK UP . . . [*pause*] BEHIND HIM! [*Emphasize each word but lower your voice with "behind him" to prep for the jump.*] And Adam was right. It was . . .

HIS SNEAKERS! [*Raise voice with the "gotcha!" jump.*]

The sole was coming off his sneakers and each time he stepped, the loose sole flapped. Adam was actually running away from . . . [*pause*] himself!

The Tinker and the Ghost

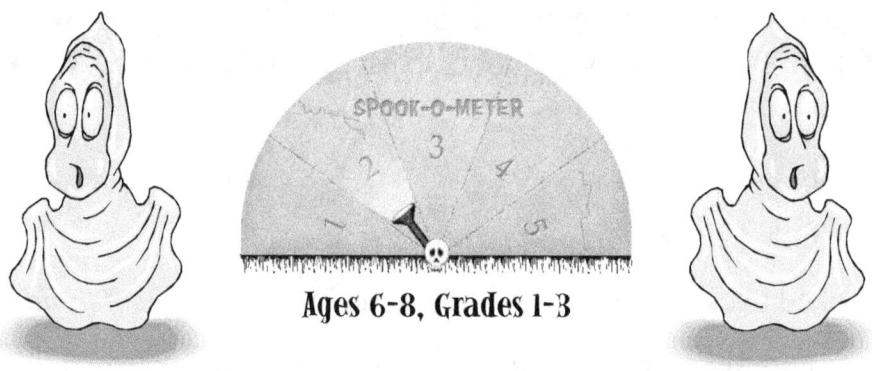

Ages 6-8, Grades 1-3

Note from Dianne: This is a fun story set in Spain that has a haunted castle, and ghost, and treasure. It's not very scary if you make the ghost a bit comical, which I like to do. The character of Esteban is cool because he is not at all bothered by the ghost. He just keeps cooking and eating. My kind of guy. LOL

Near the city of Toledo in Spain, there was an old gray castle that no one would enter because it was . . . [*pause*] HAUNTED. [*Emphasize "haunted" and make a shocked face.*]

One day, on All Hallow's Eve, a tinker named Esteban wandered into the village. In the marketplace, he learned that if he stayed overnight in the haunted castle and came out alive, the owner of the castle would give him a thousand gold *reales*! [*Rub fingers together to make the gesture for "money."*]

So Esteban packed his pots and pans, some firewood, a dozen fresh eggs, a slab of bacon, and a flask of wine. He entered the castle and it was cold and dark. [*Cup hand over eyes as if looking around.*] Once his eyes adjusted to the darkness, he spotted a large fireplace.

"Ah!" he cried. "Perfect!" He built a roaring fire and began cooking his bacon. He loved the cheerful sound and the delightful smell of sizzling bacon. [*Mime smelling bacon.*]

He lifted his flask of wine to take a swig when suddenly . . . [*pause*] a voice cried out from the fireplace,

From *Spooktacular Tales: 25 Just Scary Enough Stories* by Dianne de Las Casas. Illustrated by Soleil Lisette. Santa Barbara, CA: Libraries Unlimited. Copyright © 2016.

"I'm falling! I'm falling! Look out below!

If you are afraid, then you'd better go!" [*Invite audience to participate.*]

Esteban said, "No worries. Just please don't land in my eggs. I am quite hungry.

THUMPITY THUMP! BUMPITY BUMP! [*Invite audience to participate.*]

Another leg fell out of the chimney.

Esteban observed that it was another perfectly good leg clothed in half a pair of brown trousers. It matched the other leg and the two joined together to become a pair. Esteban took a bite of his bacon, which was now crispy.

He lifted his flask of wine to take a swig when suddenly . . . [*pause*] a voice cried out from the fireplace,

"I'm falling! I'm falling! Look out below!

If you are afraid, then you'd better go!" [*Encourage the audience to participate.*]

Esteban said, "No worries. Just please don't land in my pan. I am quite hungry.

THUMPITY THUMP! BUMPITY BUMP! [*Encourage the audience to participate.*]

A body fell out of the chimney. It was clothed in a blue shirt and a brown vest. The body went with the legs and they all joined together. Esteban cut into his egg, and the yolk oozed out onto his bacon. Yum!

He lifted his flask of wine to take a swig when suddenly . . . [*pause*] a voice cried out from the fireplace,

"I'm falling! I'm falling! Look out below!

If you are afraid, then you'd better go!" [*Encourage the audience to participate.*]

Esteban said, "No worries. Just please don't land in my food. I am quite hungry.

THUMPITY THUMP! BUMPITY BUMP! [*Encourage the audience to participate.*] Two arms fell out of the chimney. They were clothed in blue shirt sleeves. The arms went with the body. The body went with the legs and they joined all joined together. Esteban began eating the last bit of his bacon. He was curious to see . . . [*pause*]

He lifted his flask of wine to take a swig when suddenly . . . [*pause*] a voice cried out from the fireplace,

"I'm falling! I'm falling! Look out below!

If you are afraid, then you'd better go!" [*Encourage the audience to participate.*]

Esteban said, "No worries. Just please don't land in my food. I am quite hungry.

THUMPITY THUMP! BUMPITY BUMP! [*Encourage the audience to participate.*] A head fell out of the chimney. It was covered in a long beard. The head went with the rest of the body and they joined all joined together. Esteban wiped his face with his napkin. What a delicious dinner and entertainment to boot!

The ghost spoke, "You are the first person to stay until my head fell out of the chimney. Everyone else died of fright. Now you can help free me."

"How so?" asked Esteban.

"If you free the treasure, which I stole when I was alive, you will free my soul. In the courtyard, there are three [*Mime three.*] buried bags. One is filled with copper coins. It must go to the church. One is filled with silver coins. It must go to the poor. The last is filled with gold coins. That is your reward for helping me."

Esteban agreed to help the ghost. The ghost said, "Dig."

Esteban replied, "Dig yourself." So the ghost dug up the treasures. [*Mime digging.*] Esteban promised to do as the ghost asked. The ghost left behind his ghostly garments as he floated up and away. [*Mime floating up with your hand.*]

In the morning, the townsfolk were shocked to see that Esteban had survived the night. The owner of the castle paid Esteban one thousand gold *reales*. Esteban packed his pots and pans to complete the ghost's requests. He gave the copper coins to his parish church, he gave the silver coins to the poor, and he kept the gold coins, as instructed. [*Rub fingers together to make the gesture for "money."*]

With his rewards, Esteban lived a contented life and never saw another ghost again, for the rest of his days. [*Wave finger from side to side to mime "never."*]

The White Satin Gown

Ages 11-13, Middle School

Note from Dianne: "The White Satin Gown" is an urban legend that has many versions. I've added a bit of humor to the story to relieve some of the tension. Still, some kids may ask if this story is really true . . .

Tina was invited to a dance. She was so excited because this was her first high school dance. Unfortunately, Tina's mom was a single mom and she couldn't afford to buy a new dress. Tina whined and moped around. "But I really want to go to this dance, mom!" [*Act like a whiny teen. LOL*]

"Fine," her mom replied. "Let's go to the thrift shop. Maybe we can find a cute vintage dress."

Tina jumped up and down, doing a happy dance. [*Jump up and down and do a happy dance.*] She said, "Mom, you're the best!" She gave her mom a big hug. [*Hug a woman or girl in the audience.*]

At the thrift store, Tina tried on a gazillion dresses. Nothing struck her fancy. That is, nothing until her mom pulled a white satin gown from the rack. Tina screeched, "That's the one!"

Her mom looked at the price and smiled. "Yes, it is." They paid for the dress and went home. Tina didn't even try on the dress. She knew it would fit. It was different and pretty, and there was just *something* about it. [*Emphasize the word "something" in a mysterious tone.*]

On the day of the dance, her date picked her up. He complimented her. "Tina, you look like an angel in that white satin gown!" Tina smiled.

At the dance, Tina began to feel dizzy. She thought she might faint so she asked her date to take her home. When Tina arrived home, she laid down on her bed. [*Mime putting your head on a pillow.*]

The next morning, Tina's mom found her daughter as stiff as a board. She died in the white satin gown. Her mom cried and said, "My poor little angel." [*Say in a whisper but audible enough so that the audience hears it.*]

No one understood what caused Tina's death so they performed an autopsy. They discovered that Tina had been poisoned by embalming fluid. It stopped her blood from flowing. Apparently, the embalming fluid penetrated her skin as she perspired while dancing, seeping from the white satin gown she wore. The gown had been stolen off the body of a dead girl before she was buried. Then the white satin gown ended up in . . . the thrift store. [*Pause dramatically before "the thrift shop."*]

[*Lower voice and say ominously . . .*] Perhaps you should be careful where YOU shop.

Source Notes

"Aaron Kelly's Bones" was adapted from "Aaron Kelly's Bones" in *Scary Stories to Tell in the Dark* by Alvin Schwartz (New York, NY: HarperCollins Publishers, 1981), "Aaron Kelly's Bones" in *Scary Reader's Theatre* by Suzanne Barchers (Englewood, CO: Teacher Ideas Press, 1994), and "The Dancing Skeleton" on ScaryforKids.com http://www.scaryforkids.com/dancing-skeleton/

"Baba Yaga" was adapted from "The Baba Yaga" in *Best-Loved Folktales of the World* edited by Joanna Cole (New York, NY: Anchor Books by Doubleday, 1982) and "Bony Legs" in *The Scary Book* edited by Joanna Cole and Stephanie Calmenson (New York, NY: Doubleday Book, 1991).

"Bloody Mary" was adapted from childhood memories of this spooky game we played in middle school and *Favorite Scary Stories of American Children* by Richard and Judy Dockrey Young (Little Rock, AR: August House, Inc., 1990).

"Bone Soup" was adapted from versions of the folktale "Stone Soup" and "Nail Soup" in *Favorite Folktales from around the World* edited by Jane Yolen (New York, NY: Pantheon Books, 1986).

"The Brown Suit" was adapted from "The Brown Suit" in *More Scary Stories to Tell in the Dark* by Alvin Schwartz (New York, NY: HarperCollins Publishers, 1984) and "The Brown Suit" on ScaryForKids.com http://www.scaryforkids.com/brown-suit/.

"The Call from the Grave" was adapted from "The Call from the Grave" in *The Scary Story Reader* by Richard and Judy Dockrey Young (Little Rock, AR: August House Publishers, Inc., 1993) and "Phone Call from the Grave" on the BoyScoutTrail.com website http://boyscouttrail.com/content/story/phone_call_from_the_grave-991.asp.

"Creak, Crack, Bump, Thump!" was adapted from childhood memories of the story as well as a version I found online called "Creak" on UltimateCampResource.com http://www.ultimatecampresource.com/site/camp-activity/creak.html.

"The Crying Baby" was adapted from "The Rosewood Coffin" in *Favorite Scary Stories of American Children* by Richard and Judy Dockrey Young (Little Rock, AR: August House, Inc., 1990), and a true story I found while researching on the Internet about a baby who cried in the coffin at her own funeral, http://metro.co.uk/2010/08/10/baby-awoke-in-coffin-and-started-crying-at-own-funeral-476000/.

"The Curse of Pele" was adapted from childhood memories of stories of Pele from growing up in Hawaii, "The Curse of Kilauea" from *The Scary Story Reader* by Richard and Judy Dockrey Young (Little Rock, AR: August House Publishers, Inc., 1993), and "A Battle Nobody Won" from *Hawaiian Myths of Earth, Sea, and Sky* by Vivian L. Thompson (Honolulu, HI: University of Hawaii Press, 1966).

"The Ghost of John" is a story that I cobbled together from a funny childhood playground song and a story summary told to me by a student at Haslet Elementary School in Haslet, Texas.

"The Ghost with One Black Eye" was adapted from my memories of the story as a young girl, when I was in the Scouts. It's a classic "Shaggy Dog" campfire tale. One of the most fantastic versions of the story I've heard is told by professional storyteller Priscilla Howe. There is a reference to the story on PlaygroundJungle.com http://www.playgroundjungle.com/2009/12/ghost-stories-theres-only-one-room-left.html. I also like this version on BoyScoutTrail.com http://www.boyscouttrail.com/content/story/ghost_with_one_black_eye-1152.asp.

"Ginny Greenteeth," was adapted from "Green Teeth" on ScaryforKids.com http://www.scaryforkids.com/green-teeth/, "Jenny Green Teeth" from *Whistle in the Graveyard: Folktales to Chill Your Bones* (New York, NY: Viking Press, 1974), and "Jenny Green Teeth" on Archive.org http://archive.org/stream/JennyGreenTeeth/JennyGreenTeeth_djvu.txt.

"The Graveyard Bone" was adapted from "Cemetery Soup" in *Scary Stories to Tell in the Dark* by Alvin Schwartz (New York, NY: HarperCollins Publishers, 1981), "The Hairy Toe" in *Haunts & Taunts* by Jean Chapman (London, England: Award Publications Ltd., 1976), "The Big Toe" in *Scary Stories to Tell in the Dark* by Alvin Schwartz (New York, NY: HarperCollins Publishers, 1981), "The Hairy Toe" in *Scared Silly: Stories to Make You Gasp and Giggle* by Judith Bauer Stamper (New York, NY: Scholastic, Inc., 2004), "The Big Hairy Toe" in *Jackie Tales* by Jackie Torrence (New York, NY: Avon Books, Inc., 1998), and *The Teeny Tiny Woman* by Barbara Seuling (New York, NY: Viking Press, 1976).

"The Hairdo" was adapted from "The Spider in the Hairdo" in *The Vanishing Hitchhiker* by Jan Harold Brunvand (New York, NY: W.W. Norton & Company, 1981) and "The Spider in the Hairdo" in *The Big Book of Urban Legends* by Jan Harold Brunvand (New York, NY: Paradox Press 1994).

"The Hook" was adapted from "The Hook" in *Spiders in the Hairdo* by David Holt and Bill Mooney (Little Rock, AR: August House Publishers, Inc., 1999), "Hook-Arm" in *The Scary Story Reader* by Richard and Judy Dockrey Young (Little Rock, AR: August House Publishers, Inc., 1993), and "The Hook" from *The Big Book of Urban Legends* by Jan Harold Brunvand (New York, NY: Paradox Press, 1994).

"I'm Coming for Your Soul!" is an original story. I love puns and I wrote this story in the tradition of the Shaggy dog tale.

"Irish Eyes" is an original story. I had a doll collection when I was growing up and she was part of my collection. There are many stories of cursed dolls. It is a popular motif that can even be seen in the movies. Here is one I found on CampfireMarshmallows.com http://www.campfiremarshmallows.com/campfire-stories/truely-scary/#story2.

"It Floats!" was adapted from "It Floats" in *The Scary Story Reader* by Richard and Judy Dockrey Young (Little Rock, AR: August House Publishers, Inc., 1993) and a reference to the story on PlaygroundJungle.com http://www.playgroundjungle.com/2009/12/ghost-stories-theres-only-one-room-left.html.

"La Llorona" (The Wailing Woman) was adapted from "La Llorona" in *The Scary Story Reader* by Richard and Judy Dockrey Young (Little Rock, AR: August House Publishers, Inc., 1993), "La Llorona" in *Ghost Stories from the American Southwest: Over 140 Spine-Tingling Tales* by Richard and Judy Dockrey Young (Little Rock, AR: August House Publishers, Inc., 1991), and "La Llorona" on AmericanFolklore.net by S. E. Schlosser http://americanfolklore.net/folklore/2012/07/the_wailing_woman_la_llorona.html and http://americanfolklore.net/folklore/2010/07/la_llorona.html.

"Over in the Graveyard" is an original remake using the pattern of the folk song, "Over in the Meadow."

"Pulling the Pumpkin" was an adapted version of a Russian folktale. I gave it a Halloween twist. One of my favorite versions of this story is *The Turnip* by Janina Domanska (London: The MacMillan Company, 1969). There is also "The Enormous Turnip" on StoriestoGrowby.com http://www.storiestogrowby.com/stories/turnip_russia.html.

"The Sack Filled with Treats" is an original story based on the structure of the Mother Goose tale, "The House That Jack Built." I was also inspired by another spooky version called "The Trunk Full of Treats" in *Scared Silly: Stories to Make You Gasp and Giggle* by Judith Bauer Stamper (New York, NY: Scholastic, Inc., 1993).

"Sneakers" was adapted from childhood memories of the tale as well as a version called "Who's Following Me" in *The Scary Story Reader* by Richard and Judy Dockrey Young (Little Rock, AR: August House Publishers, Inc., 1993).

"The Tinker and the Ghost" was adapted from "The Tinker and the Ghost" in *Haunting: Ghosts and Ghouls from around the World* by Margaret Hodges (Canada: Little, Brown and Company, 1991), "The Tinker and the Ghost" in *Favorite Folktales from around the World* edited by Jane Yolen (New York, NY: Pantheon Books, 1986), and a version from

New Mexico called "The Skeleton" on AmericanFolklore.Net http://americanfolklore.net/folklore/2011/07/the_skeleton.html.

"The White Satin Gown" was adapted from "The White Satin Evening Gown" in "*Scary Stories to Tell in the Dark* by Alvin Schwartz (New York, NY: HarperCollins Publishers, 1981), "The White Dress" in *The Scary Story Reader* by Richard and Judy Dockrey Young (Little Rock, AR: August House Publishers, Inc., 1993), and "The Deadly Dress" in *Spiders in the Hairdo* by David Holt and Bill Mooney (Little Rock, AR: August House Publishers, Inc., 1999).

Web Resources

Besides the books I have listed in my Source Notes, these are great web resources for spooky stories!

American Folklore.net

AmericanFolklore.net is a treasure trove of stories. The site has a great section on scary stories from all over the United States.

http://www.americanfolklore.net/spooky-stories.html

Boy Scout Trail

A great site for Scouts! There are a number of spooky stories on the site. I love the search feature you can use to find a scary story.

http://www.boyscouttrail.com

Campfire Stories

Want classic campfire stories? This site has them and they are even categorized into "Legends," "Scary," and "Funny."

http://www.ultimatecampresource.com/site/camp-activities/campfire-stories.html

Scary Stories

A wonderful site filled with tons of scary stories from around the world.

http://www.scarystories.ca/

About the Author and Illustrator

Dianne de Las Casas is an award-winning author, storyteller, and founder of Picture Book Month. Her performances, dubbed "revved-up storytelling," are full of energetic audience participation. The author of 25 books, Dianne was the International Reading Association LEADER 2014 Poet Laureate, and the 2014 recipient of the Ann Martin Book Mark Award. Her children's titles include *The Cajun Cornbread Boy*, *There's a Dragon in the Library*, *The Little "Read" Hen*, *The House That Santa Built*, and *Cinderellaphant*. She is the proud mom of culinary celebrity, Kid Chef Eliana, and illustrator Soleil Lisette.

Visit Dianne's website at diannedelascasas.com. Visit Picture Book Month at PictureBookMonth.com. Twitter & Instagram: @AuthorDianneDLC. Facebook: fanofdianne.

Soleil Lisette is a graphic designer and illustrator who has illustrated several books including Dianne de Las Casas's ABC-Clio titles: *Scared Silly: 25 Tales to Tickle and Thrill*, *Tell Along Tales: Playing with Participation Stories*, and *Stories on Board: Creating Board Games from Favorite Tales*. She lives in Baton Rouge, Louisiana, where she works for a boutique design firm.

www.ingramcontent.com/pod-product-compliance
Lightning Source LLC
Chambersburg PA
CBHW080940300426
44115CB00017B/2897